"Reading Gary's stories aloud has become a new family ritual. When the kids see me laughing while I'm reading, they know they're in for a treat at dinnertime."

—Bill Corry, one of Florida's "Super Lawyers" and *Florida Trend*'s "Legal Elite"

"A Gary Yordon column means a banner day guaranteed to produce an endorphin boost . . . His verbatim accounts of phone conversations with his parents are always good for a belly laugh."

—Marjorie R. Turnbull, former Florida state representative

DRIVING THE
ROAD OF LIFE
WITH A FLAT TIRE

Walli —

Hope Your

Enjoy

the

Ride

DRIVING THE ROAD OF LIFE WITH A FLAT TIRE

Stories from My Mistake-Filled Life

Gary Yordon

Some of these essays were previously published in the *Tallahassee Democrat* newspaper, owned by Gannett Co., Inc.—most in different form.

Published by Quill, an imprint of Inkshares, Inc.,
San Francisco, California
www.inkshares.com

Cover design by Sean Whitson and Stephen Leacock

© Dave Barfield
© justinkendra/iStockPhoto

ISBN: 9781942645474
e-ISBN: 9781942645481
Library of Congress Control Number: 2016945075

First edition

Printed in the United States of America

To my endlessly interesting and profoundly patient life partner, Berneice Cox

CONTENTS

FOREWORD

Diminished Capacity is an obscure Alan Alda movie based on the book by Sherwood Kiraly. In the movie, a mentally diminished Alda ties fishing line to each key of an old manual typewriter and secures it to the end of a dock with each line dipping into the Mississippi River. Whatever the fish put to paper is the sum and substance of what Kiraly called fish poetry. When I think about how I write, I can't quite get the process of fish poetry out of my head. I get an idea in my head, sit down, and start dipping my fingers in the water.

I'm not a writer by trade. I'm chagrined when I'm around real writers. I imagine they studied writing, that they live and breathe writing and have little patience for those who call themselves writers without all the proper credentials. I figure they have inside writing jokes that nonwriters will never get. I feel like I'm a vacuum cleaner salesman at a Tupperware party. Sure, I can chat about getting your house in order, but when they bring up the vintage four-piece Servalier Nesting Canister Set with Lids, I'm out of my league.

It never mattered to me because after forty years in television, writing a book was not part of the plan—that is, until a slimy visitor stopped by our house. A few years ago I came home from a vacation and found a giant snake in our bedroom (later photos confirmed it was about eighteen inches, but that's not really the issue here). My first thought was to sell the house, but I quickly realized that would mean cleaning the garage, so I was forced to execute plan B: removing the beast. I survived the encounter and decided to share the epic battle in our local newspaper. The response from readers was overwhelming, and before I knew it I had editors calling to ask if I was a one-hit wonder. My response was, "Yes, of course, but if you're talking about more writing, then sure, I have more to say."

So while I'm not a classically trained writer, I am a classically trained talker. I pretty much write like I talk. At first I tried being a really clever writer, but I failed miserably. Mary Ann Lindley is a former newspaper editor who is a good friend and a patient teacher. Before I sent my written words out into the universe, I asked her to look over a few sample columns and let me know what she thought. What she gave back to me looked like someone had put red ink on a chicken's feet and had it walk all over the paper. She was smart enough to tell me to quit trying to be Shakespeare and just tell folks what's on my mind. In one particular early draft of a column, I wrote about a friend who had built a car from scratch. I wrote, "The gearshift knob was covered in leather and pride." Mary Ann told me it was just covered in leather. That one simple lesson turned me loose. Just talk on paper. I can do that.

Soon I had a regular column and discovered the absurdity of my everyday life had touched a nerve with readers. I realized those things I put in print were the same adventures my readers ran into in their everyday lives—with a few twists and turns added. I'm a hypochondriac who believes the Internet was invented to check symptoms. I'm not allowed to touch power tools, but that hasn't stopped me. Home repair is forbidden, but I'm convinced that with enough duct tape and pliers I can repair the space shuttle. I fear death and have left strict instructions that if all that's left of me is a finger, my family is to keep it alive in case they find a way to attach an entire body to a living finger. My car is stocked like a bomb shelter so I can survive any incident, like being trapped in a car wash. I don't hunt because I can't find camouflage gear in a fabric that doesn't itch. I fear heights, clowns, tall bridges, deep water, and MRIs (or any other tight space that makes me feel like I'm being loaded into a torpedo tube).

Basically, I'm all of you—just a guy driving the road of life with a flat tire. My stories are about the adventures we face every day. They're about urologists with big hands and assembly directions with small type. Things I wish I hadn't eaten and ceiling fans I shouldn't have tried to repair. Endless absurd discussions with my ninety-year-old Jewish mother, my gentle giant of a father, and the plethora of innocently bad advice given to my children. If your idea of camping is venturing out as far as your longest extension cord, then I'm your writer. If you think the power is shut off to a light fixture just because you turned off the wall switch, then we are on the same page.

You will get to know my amazingly patient wife, Berneice, a woman who has mastered the art of shaking her head in disbelief at the things I manage to stumble into. When I start a home project, Berneice expects to find me crumpled at the base of the ladder, so she's learned to not overreact to the thud. She graciously absorbs my foolishness and seems to have accepted her reality, although I'm consistently amazed each day to come home and find her still here. I've never quite been able to figure out what she's thinking through our many adventures, but that's the beauty of Berneice—after more than a quarter century together, I still barely even know her. Layer after layer of complicated woman, and I wouldn't have it any other way. Berneice is my life adventure.

We have three children in our blended family: Zachary, who passed away a few years ago; Dustin; and Jackson. Jackson is the acorn who didn't fall far from my tree. Neither one of us should be allowed to hold a hammer. Jackson is funny, smart, and creative—three excellent life qualities. Mostly he has a great big heart. He cares about things most of us should but don't. Dustin takes after his mom, thank God—smart, engaging, and spiritually connected to his universe. Dustin will challenge you to examine those things in life you thought you had figured out. Both are great guys and even better fathers. I'll share a few thoughts about Zachary in this book and pray they do justice to his gentle soul. Zach was profoundly challenged and through it all taught us what really mattered in this life.

If you come along on this ride, there will be laughs, tears, and everything in between. I can promise my book will be an easy read. It's a collection of my columns with bits of commentary about why each one popped into the playground I call my head.

While most columns have appeared in magazines and newspapers, a few in this book are not quite suited for general audiences. (Hey, not every adventure is G-rated.)

If you're an English teacher reading this book, plan ahead and schedule some couch time with your favorite therapist, because I'm not very good at following the writing rules.

I'd be stunned if my book makes its way out of your bathroom but would be thrilled if it bangs into your funny bone. There may even be a few things that cause you to step back and look at where you are. So check your tires and enjoy the ride.

GIANT SNAKE

This was the column that started my writing journey. Like a baseball player's first hit, it will always have special meaning to me. But instead of a ball on my mantel, I'll just have to settle for a big chunk of shame.

I heard the version of my name where the *y* at the end of "Gary" lasted about five seconds. Unlike the three-second version, which means one of the kids did something wrong, or the two-second version, which means we need to talk, the five-second version means something cataclysmic has occurred and requires immediate attention.

We had just returned home from a weekend at the beach. I went into the great room. Berneice went into the bedroom. Big mistake. Berneice came face-to-face with the most unwelcome of visitors: a snake.

I reached the bedroom doorway, and there I saw the beast. At first glance he appeared to be about ten feet long. As I caught my breath, I realized it was closer to five feet. (Later photos would confirm a length of about eighteen inches, but that's not the issue here.)

The first thing I did was grab my big cooler and put it over the snake, trapping it until I could think this through.

I quickly weighed my options: 1) Sell the house. 2) Call for help. 3) Deal with the beast myself. Option 1 required moving my entertainment system, so it was dismissed. Option 3 was never a realistic consideration, so option 2 it was.

I have always believed that one of the top five reasons to have children is to help remove snakes from the house, so it was finally going to pay off. We called our geographically closest boy, Dustin. Unfortunately, he and his wife, Ashley, were driving back from Jacksonville and were still 150 miles away. Later he admitted that even if he was on the couch it would not have mattered—he didn't do snakes.

So I called my go-to guy and baseball teammate, Chip Campbell, who lives just around the corner from our home. After promising him beer and food, he agreed to come help. Twenty minutes later he showed up at my front door in full catcher's gear. Seriously. Mask, chest protector, shin guards, and a broom. I started to laugh but then got it. "Good call, Chippy."

Chip and I moved to the bedroom to survey the crisis. Immediately we realized the opaque cooler meant we could not see what the snake was doing. Was he casually enjoying the darkness or testing the perimeters for a weakness? We quickly realized we needed visual confirmation.

A piece of glass covering a piece of wall art seemed right. My plan was to carefully slide it under the cooler while getting the snake positioned on top of the glass. Then we'd flip over the cooler, dropping the snake to the bottom and having the ability to see through the improvised glass top.

As I started to carefully slip the glass under the cooler, I asked Chip to get ready to help me flip it over. From behind the bathroom door I heard Chip say, "I didn't hear that!" Okay, I'm utterly alone. So I start slipping the glass under, not realizing the tension I was putting on the cooler—and the glass breaks. Now I've got broken glass and a snake.

We needed another plan. We needed a see-through box. That way I could just lift up the cooler and Chip could replace it with the new box. We found a hard plastic hatbox and started planning the switch.

Logistics had to be carefully considered. After applying a cold compress to Chip's forehead, we rehearsed the moves. I would pull off the cooler, and Chip would replace it with the hatbox. Chip asked why I would be moving away from the snake and he would be moving toward it. I convinced him that the snake was after me, not him, and that seemed to work. In the distance I could hear Berneice booking a room at Hotel Duval.

The moment had arrived. The moment our ancestors prepared us for when they were dragging their knuckles around a campfire. All our instincts and senses would be in play. I looked at Chip, and he looked back through the catcher's mask—an unspoken man-to-man communication. It was "go" time.

What happened next was a blur of hands, feet, broom, and baseball gear. To this day I don't remember exactly what occurred. I just know the snake was in the hatbox and Chip and I were still alive.

We let the fog clear and looked at each other with glazed eyes, and after a brief silence we did what men do: jumped up, bumped chests, and yelled, "YEAH, BABY!"

Killing the snake seemed unnecessarily cruel, so we carried the hatbox out far enough away from the house—about a mile past Cleveland, Ohio—to ensure that the snake would not come back.

I'm confident over time as I share this tale with my grandchildren that the snake will indeed be every bit of ten feet. It will have developed a rattle and large fangs. That's the nature of snake stories, and I'm sticking to mine.

CAR WINDOWS

I was on this call for ten seconds, and I knew I'd be writing about it. Sometimes you just need to not think, to just take notes.

My first mistake is getting my ninety-year-old father an iPhone. My second mistake is answering his call while he is buying his first new car in thirty years.

You would like Anne and Lenny Yordon. Mom is five foot nothing and pretty much Jewish Mother 101. Dad is a big bear of a man and the sweetest guy on the planet. They've been married for sixty-one years, and I'd be hard pressed to remember a day when we didn't laugh. Picture the Seinfelds, and you've got it.

Within minutes of their latest visit, Dad peels me off to the side and asks me to help persuade Mom to let him buy a new car. It seems she doesn't want to cut into our inheritance. Trying to get my mother to change her mind is like trying to get a beaver to take down a dam. I tell her that, if she didn't agree, I'd take the cost of the car and stuff it in her urn. Her eye rolling is so extreme her hair moves, but she caves. Let the adventure begin.

Four days later I get a call from my dad. He's at a dealership in Daytona, sitting in the front seat of the car he wants to get. My phone rings, and I'm about to lose twenty minutes of my life.

Dad: *I'm sitting in the front seat of this new car, and I love it. It's got Bluetooth and a satellite.*

It may as well have bubblegum seats and a gingerbread steering wheel because Dad will never figure out how to use the gadgets.

Me: *That's great, Dad. Does Mom like it?*

Dad: *Your son wants to know if you like it.*

Mom: (yelling from the passenger seat) *It's okay, but I can't see out the window.*

Me: (reluctantly asking the question I know will make me want to fill my ears with cement) *Dad, why can't she see out the window?*

Dad: *Gary wants to know why you can't see out the window.*

Mom: (yelling) *I'm too short. My eyes only come up to the top of the door.*

Dad: *She says she's too short—and she can't find the button that fixes the seat. Here, you talk to her.*

Me: *No, Dad, don't hand her the ph . . . Hi, Mom.*

Mom: *If I bend my neck and pull myself up with this handle, I can see outside. I can see the second floor of everything we pass. He really wants this car.*

Me: *Mom, there's a button for that. Give the phone to Dad and reach down on the side of the seat and find the button.*

At this point Mom drops the phone between the seats, but I'm still connected and hear everything.

Mom: (yelling as seat goes into full recline) *Oh Lord! I'm stuck.*

Dad: *I can't reach the phone.*

Mom: *Lenny, I can't get back up.*

Me: (laughing so hard I can't breathe) *I'm still here!*

Mom: *Lenny, I really can't get up. I can't reach the button.*

Dad: *The damn phone is wedged down here.*

Mom: *Is Gary still on the phone?*

Dad: *How the hell would I know if he's still on the phone. GARY, ARE YOU STILL THERE? If he's there, I can't hear him.*

Mom: *Where is our salesman? I need him to do this seat.*

Dad: *Maybe I should call him.*

Mom: *That's not funny. I'm really stuck here.*

Dad: *Do you have anything in your purse I can use to pry this phone up?*

Mom: *For the love of God, I can't reach my purse.*

I hear rustling noises, and then the phone goes dead. One minute later I get a call from Dad, who has accidentally hit FaceTime, which he doesn't know exists on his phone, and I watch him trying to hang up because he thinks it's just the camera.

Me: (yelling) *Dad, it's not the camera. It's FaceTime—I'm here!*

Dad: (who has just put the phone to his ear) *How are you here on the camera?*

Me: (looking into my dad's ear) *Move the phone away from your ear so I can see you.*

Mom: *Lenny, give me the phone. Gary, it's Mom.*

Me: (now looking in my mom's ear) *I know, Mom.*

Mom: *Who makes a car like this where you can't see out the window?*

Dad: *Who makes a wife who's four feet tall?*

Me: *Dad, you can't get a car if Mom can't see out the window.*

Dad: *It's not like there's anything out there she needs to see.*

Mom: *So what, you want me to get taller?*

Me: *Guys, I think you should look for another car. I'm sure there's one with a window Mom can use.*

Dad: *Maybe they can lower the windows?*

Me: *Do they have a button that lets you unhear a conversation?*

NEAR-DEATH EXPERIENCE

I am—without question—my own worst enemy, but something is going to kill me. That much I know. True hypochondria demands vigilance. If I am nothing else, I am vigilant.

I recently went for my annual physical. As the nurse was walking me to my room, my doctor emerged from another room and told me to go with her and that he would come by and stick his head in. I thought to myself, "Wow, this really is going to be a thorough checkup."

Most men don't like to admit that they worry about their health. I revel in my concern. I have made hypochondria an art form. I am the Monet of medical misery.

When I see an advertisement for some disorder, I can develop the symptoms within minutes. At restaurants I order the dish that's least likely to choke me. I pick my doctor by the size of his hands. You get a big-handed urologist, and it's like you backed into a Buick. In the air force, they won't let a pilot in the cockpit if they're too big, but a urologist can have a meat hook on the end of his arm and get licensed.

Turning sixty is not for the faint of heart. If you wake up in the morning and there's not a finger lying on your pillow, it's a victory—another day and nothing fell off. Parts of you that used to be in one place are now someplace else. You make noises that you never made before. If you have hair, it's receding like a low tide, and "grits" defines your biceps more than it does your breakfast.

Then there's the whole memory thing. You walk into a room and have no idea why. Thirty seconds ago you had a reason for going there, but that's long gone. You figure it will come back to you if you just stay there for a minute. Last night I stood in front of my open refrigerator like I was waiting for the food to talk. I had a point to make here, but it has slipped away.

I'm convinced the Internet was invented so we could check symptoms. Recently I woke up in the middle of the night with a ringing in my ears. WebMD, here I come. I figure, despite the zero minutes I spent in med school, I can figure this one out.

Here's where it gets a little tricky. It says the ringing could be anything from too much wax to a stroke. So I have two choices: gently probe with a Q-tip or immediately call 911. The problem is that as soon as I read the word "stroke," I start to develop new symptoms. Now I'm on to other symptoms, and while I'm reading I'm pretty sure my left arm is going numb. I'll Google "heart attack symptoms" in a moment; right now I'm dealing with my impending stroke.

The description says I should try to smile because failure to do so is one of the warning signs of a stroke. So there I am at 3:00 a.m., sitting in my living room with the bells of St. Mary's going off in my ears and likely only moments to live, trying to muster a smile. I wonder if this is how my wife is going to find me: stiff as a board on the floor with a half smile on my face.

My symptoms are now multiplying like rabbits—cold sweats and what feels like a swollen gland in my neck. I'm having trouble swallowing, and my eyes are burning. Just then I'm distracted by a pop-up ad for gout medication. Great, now my foot hurts. Suddenly I realize the Cubs will never have won in my lifetime and, oh yeah, I'll never see my kids again.

It's all spinning out of control, and then I have this lucid moment of logic: I've been reading all this for an hour. If it were any of the bad things, they would have already happened. Slowly my symptoms begin to dissipate. Maybe the ringing is just wax. I regain feeling in my left arm.

That was a close one.

Fast-forward to my physical. It went great, although I'm not 100 percent certain it was *my* blood they tested. Those things get mixed up sometimes. I make a mental note to make sure I get a second blood test just to make sure the first test was accurate.

I had one more thing I wanted to share with you. Give me a minute. It'll come to me.

TEARS AND CHICK FLICKS

Sure, try and tell me you haven't had this happen to you. Go ahead, I dare you.

He sweeps her into his arms, and they gaze at each other like two pumas. His hand reaches around to the small of her back and pulls her close. The wind picks up, and the rain begins to fall. They kiss. Not a little peck but an excruciatingly long kiss. A kiss that lingers like passed gas in an elevator.

Our decision to watch a movie starts simple enough with Berneice and me perusing the pay-per-view choices on a cozy Sunday night. I see what's coming, and I make a futile attempt to distract her as *The Notebook* passes on the screen. Like a moth to a flame she sees it, and I know I'm about to lose three hours of my life.

Author Nicholas Sparks is the bucking bronco of the chick-flick / love-story rodeo. I imagine if I ever met Sparks that I would get a hug instead of a handshake, and it would last uncomfortably long. Eleven of his books have been turned into sap-dripping movies. *The Notebook* is the most painful of them all.

Sparks's movies generally start with the unbridled passion of forbidden love and end sixty years later with the forbidden love couple lying in a bed and sweetly dying in each other's arms. The formula is pretty basic: the forbidden guy has a Harley 750 instead of a 401(k). The perfect girl meets him when her parents' Bentley has a flat tire on the way to her cotillion. She's supposed to have her first dance with a stuffy and equally wealthy guy named Chip, but when she bumps into torn-T-shirt guy, it's all over. Let the forbidden begin.

Think of a really bad 1970s movie with an overplayed, super-slow-motion death scene. The one where a guy gets shot and turns to the wall so he can slowly slide down to the floor. Then he starts to get up and is shot again, and he spins to land on the bed where he bounces up and lunges only to be shot again as he flops onto the dresser. Looking at the camera, he extends his hand only to be shot again, and he's back to sliding down the wall. Now take that and imagine it's a kiss instead of a gunshot, and you get Nicholas Sparks.

So when Berneice looks over and suggests *The Notebook*, I react like a real man should: "Sure, babe, it looks like a good one." Her job is to sit back and enjoy the movie. My work has just begun. I've got three hours of looking sensitive in front of me, and I know it's going to take every bit of focus I can muster.

Even worse, I know there will be a key moment at the end when she looks over at me and I damn sure better have some moisture in my eyes—maybe not a tear but certainly some general, perceivable wetness.

I figured the big sad ending was about ten minutes away, so it was time to consider my options. My plan was to recall a surefire moment of misery. I started by remembering when I was fifteen and was the only kid who wore a costume to a

Halloween party. I hopped in wearing a bunny suit while all my friends were making out. I recalled the shame but couldn't muster up any eye moisture. The clock was ticking. And then it hit me: the 2003 playoff game when the Marlins beat the Cubs because a fan got in the way of the ball. That was it. I could feel the moisture around my left eye. There was no more time. It would have to do. I covered by rubbing my right eye.

Berneice looked over sweetly, and I looked back like a pound puppy. She had that "he gets it" look in her eyes. All was well.

Note to Sparks: It would be helpful if the elderly lovers died holding hands in box seats at a Cubs game. But if they absolutely have to be in a bed together, can they at least wear bunny suits?

CATFISHING

I love the idea of doing dad things with my boys. While I'm not very good at most of them, it hasn't stopped me from diving in. This one had real potential but turned ugly in a hurry—just another emotional scar on our children's psyche.

The kitten was thrashing so much I couldn't get a grip. My son was screaming. "We killed the kitty!" It was not a good fishing trip.

I really wanted to be a fisherman. Fishing seems so serene. Facebook is filled with people proudly holding their catch: sixty-pound kids holding sixty-five-pound groupers and women cradling mackerels like slimy babies. It never locked in for me. I've come to accept that I'm an excellent fish cooker but an impatient and unskilled fish catcher.

My dad didn't fish. We bonded over the smoked salmon on our bagels. But somehow my lack of interest didn't stop me from feeling an obligation to do the father–son fishing thing. Fathers and sons dipping a line was a Norman Rockwell rite of passage, so I was determined to have that iconic moment with my son. We were going to fish, no matter how much it hurt.

My son and I were going to cast our hopes and dreams into the great wet void. We were going to talk about girls, the Cubs, and all things men. We were going to dangle our feet over the end of the dock and share a peanut butter and jelly sandwich. The fact that my son Jackson was three years old didn't diminish my enthusiasm for conversation. It did, however, slightly alter the subject matter. It was a bright Saturday morning when I decided this would be the day we bonded over bass. The dangling and the sandwich sharing were going to happen.

We lived in a small but quaint little neighborhood on the east side of town called Twin Lakes. I surmised that there had to be at least one fish in those lakes. Actually, the "lakes" were two big stormwater ponds, but no one was going to buy a home in a place called "Twin Stormwater Ponds."

I ran to Walmart and picked up two Ronco fishing sets. Everything was in one package—a rod and reel with fishing line already attached and a couple of hooks. There was even a little instruction book with a picture of a dad and a kid. It was perfect.

I realized when we were ready to go that I had forgotten to get bait. I had failed to pick up an Uncle Josh Pork Frog or even a Rapala Hoola Popper. (I just Googled those fishing lure names to give real fishermen a reason to keep reading.) All I had in the fridge was salami, and I remember thinking, "Who doesn't like salami?"

We hit the dock, and I began to tie the hooks to the line. First mine. I got it set up and put a chunk of salami on the hook and moved to set up Jackson's rig. It was then that I heard a shriek behind me so shrill the written word can't do it justice. I spun around to see that a kitten had wandered onto the dock and taken the salami bait.

I had caught a kitten.

Even I knew the fishing rule for kittens was catch and release. I quickly realized the options for removing a hook from a kitten's mouth were limited. It would be easier to try and grab a marble in a blender. The kitten took off, dragging the pole behind. In hot pursuit, I realized that if I grabbed the pole I would set the hook deeper, a good strategy if you were kitten fishing but not so good when you're trying to save face in front of your three-year-old. So I ran past the pole and leaped for the catch of the day.

The actual hook removal plan for a freaked-out cat is similar to the classic wrestling-six-rats-in-a-wool-sweater process. Basically, you just keep swinging until it's mercifully over. It was a blur of paws, claws, and salami—all to the tune of Jackson screaming, "We killed the kitty!" When the fur settled, I just lay there for a moment confirming that I still had both ears. The kitty ran away, but we were now blood brothers. When I opened my eyes, Jackson was standing over me, asking innocently if we were done fishing.

Uh, yes.

That was the day I made the decision to bond over baseball instead of fishing. The odds of swinging a bat and not hitting a kitten seemed better. Jackson and I haven't fished since that fateful day on the docks, but we've played a lot of catch. And talked about girls, the Cubs, and all things men. But to this day I still cannot eat catfish.

GHOSTS OF JOHN DENHAM

Berneice and I love little adventures. This was one we'd had on our agenda for a long time when we finally decided to peek into the great beyond.

The eight of us traversed the stairway to the windowed cupola. One by one, we wound our way up the narrow, twisted collection of 144-year-old wooden steps. It was the cupola where the ghost of John Denham had been seen most frequently. The air was heavy with the stench of fear. Or it could have been my sneakers. Either way, we were ready to come face-to-face with the unknown.

I'm not sure how I feel about ghosts. I'm one of those folks who doesn't believe or disbelieve without concrete evidence. I've talked to enough credible people who have had strange, unexplained experiences and have no reason to embellish, so my mind is open and perhaps even hopeful.

When it comes to ghosts, I carefully avoid the religious connotation. It strikes me that the church has always had a narrow and conflicting view of ghosts: when our physical bodies die, our spirits emerge—either heading north or south—and if they hang around here, then they are deemed demonic. It seems earthbound spirits should have hired Casper's PR firm.

Frightfully small, Monticello, Florida, is generally regarded as one of the most haunted towns in America. Monticellians pride themselves on their spooky reputation. Bizarre things seem to happen there all the time. But this column is not about their local government—it's about their haunted houses. The John Denham House is on the national register of officially haunted travel destinations. It's a lovely B&B carefully managed by the un-spooky Pat Inmon.

My wife and I, along with three other couples, had finally decided to spend a Saturday night getting the bejesus scared out of us. We cruised over late in the afternoon and checked into the Denham House to begin our ghost adventure.

We carefully considered our plan to engage with the great beyond. First, we started drinking wine. Then we had more wine. Finally, we had more wine.

We were ready.

We hired a wonderful woman who gives a walking ghost tour of the entire town for $15 a head. (The head must be attached to a living body.) She was dressed in antebellum garb with one hand holding up her malfunctioning hoop skirt and the other a spooky lantern. We were grateful for both hands.

She walked us by the elementary school where late at night children could be heard laughing and lights could be seen dancing through the hallways. Then she showed us a house where they've never been able to get the blood off the wall after a murder had been committed there. Rumor is that they replaced the wall and the blood showed up again. As we moved to the next location, we passed the tax collector's office, and we all agreed that was the scariest place we had seen.

After cutting the walking tour short, mostly because we were having trouble walking, we decided it was time to go face-to-face with the dead Denham, and his equally dead family, so we headed back to the B&B. We were warned that actual sightings were rare. A "visit" would more likely feel like a cold breeze on the neck or a glancing shadow sweeping by. Chances of Denham popping up and asking for the car keys were slim.

We made our way up to the cupola, sat down, and waited. And waited. And waited some more. I finally did feel something on the back of my neck—a mosquito. But, in fairness, it might have been the tiny ghost of an already dead mosquito.

Finally, we all retreated to our rooms and slipped into bed, leaving one eye open. Berneice woke me at 2:00 a.m. because she heard a light knocking. I thought I heard it too. Then came what Berneice described as a "whoosh" sound near the stairs. And then sleep.

We woke at first light to the aroma of breakfast being prepared. We pinched each other just to make sure we were still among the living. We all agreed that the possibility of seeing a ghost was as good as actually seeing one. Good wine and good friends. Time to find out where Denham left the car keys.

KIDNEY STONE

If you've had one, you get it. If you haven't, then you can gain a greater understanding of this column if you go to your toolbox, take out a hammer, and smack your big toe while you read this.

I was on the eleventh hole when I felt a twinge in my right side. I didn't think too much of it because I was, in fact, swinging a golf club. By the next hole, despite all my stretching, I couldn't work it out. A few minutes later, the pain really settled in. Five more minutes, and I was in agony.

As my golf partner Scott loaded me onto our cart and headed back to the clubhouse, the other two guys in our foursome (none of them doctors) concluded that it was my appendix. They called for an ambulance, while Scott called a friend at a nearby hospital ER and told him to be on the lookout for me.

Through the fog of my pain, I remember that call, because right after Scott told the ER guy that I was being brought by ambulance for what looked like a burst appendix, there was a pause as he listened intently. I imagined that Scott was being given important lifesaving information. After a few seconds of intense listening, Scott answered, "Two under par with seven holes left to play." Okay, fair enough.

By now the pain was unbearable. Something from another planet had crawled into me and was stabbing me with photon darts. In the emergency room, the doctor saw me in the fetal position asking for my mommy. He didn't touch me—just looked at the nurse and said the two words friends had warned me about for years: "Kidney stones." Apparently he had seen this before.

If you've never had a kidney stone, let me help you understand the journey. Imagine trying to stuff a porcupine through a garden hose. That's pretty much what it's like trying to pass a kidney stone. I know women who have had children are rolling their eyes right about now. Look, I'll give you childbirth. The general theory of trying to push something big through a small space is a given. I'm not suggesting giving birth is a walk in the park. But a kidney stone is like a baby with moose antlers. You'd have a better chance shoving a shot put through a sausage casing. After two hours, I would have gladly traded my stone for a baby. There is no position that relieves the pain. There is no heating pad to ease the poking.

The stone laughed at morphine.

It was about three hours into the torture-fest when all of a sudden the pain went away. I hugged three nurses and a guy lying on a gurney in the hallway. I offered to buy a round of Demerol for the house. I was Julie Andrews running through a Salzburg meadow.

Was this it? Is it over that fast? Where did it go? It didn't take long for the doctor to burst my glee bubble. He told me I was in the eye of the hurricane. The stone had just stopped moving and would most likely get going again soon. It did—with a vengeance. It's as if the stone caught it's spiky, demon-like breath and started up again. And then the obvious hit me: there's only one way out. This was not going to be pleasant.

Five hours and sixty-seven explicit M*#*$#$@#*s later, the stone finally passed. It actually didn't look very fierce. It was smaller than I expected (although it almost had to be, because I was thinking "Buick"). I took it home and later glued it inside the wooden-block mouth of a nutcracker soldier and gave it to my friend Bo as a gift.

I dedicate this column to all the brave kidney stone survivors. You are not alone. We are a club united. So the next time you're pretzeled in pain, and the slightest murmur from a family member makes your head spin around like Linda Blair, remember these sacred words: this too shall pass.

$150 WORDS

I appear to be classier because Berneice is in my life. Actually I haven't changed much, but she surrounds me with things that are classy, so ipso facto I look classier. Her attempt to upgrade our space led to this column.

Four little words—harmless by themselves, but together they totaled $600. That's $150 per word. Just four little words: 1) Hey . . . 2) how . . . 3) about . . . 4) Costco.

When Berneice and I first met, my finest piece of art was a stunning five-foot-tall black-velvet Elvis. I also had a really nice 3-D Last Supper, where the disciples' eyes followed you around the room. I had a few tasteful John Wayne pieces, including a stagecoach clock, but the Elvis was really the star of the show.

Berneice has impeccable taste (if you don't count choosing me). She's not snobby about art or fashion, but she has a really good eye. It took us six months and every furniture store between Tallahassee and Atlanta to buy just the right leather sofa. She can see art on the wall before the art is on the wall. Our home is a reflection of her good taste. I'm smart enough to know that the only thing between a flea market family room and me is Berneice.

We've had words about the 3-D Last Supper. It's been in the attic for twenty-five years, and I still believe it has a place somewhere in our home. There's this empty wall space above a closet door at the top of the stairs leading to our guest room. I can't imagine a more perfect place for such a mesmerizing masterpiece. She can: the attic.

I am not throwing all men under the esthetic bus here—just me. I know plenty of guys who have really good taste when it comes to home design. Hey, I like a good-looking sofa as much as the next guy. But there are places I think most men are just fine with function and not so caught up in design. Which brings me to patio furniture.

I never thought patio furniture was a big deal. I mean it's patio furniture. I'm not saying we should flip a cooler upside down and use it as a table, but it's outside furniture. It's designed to get soaked, baked, chipped, and frozen. That's its job. I'm not taking a nap on it, and if the governor stops by for brunch, we're probably using the dining room. In a few months, there'll be a wasps' nest under a chair and citronella candle wax all over the tabletop.

Berneice believes patio furniture is an extension of the home. Look: deep down I know she's right, so I'm trying to find the least expensive extension of the home. A few weeks ago we started the search for just the right outdoor dining set.

We went to a dozen stores, and nothing caught her eye until we stumbled on a set she kind of liked. I could sense she was beginning to wear down, so I seized the moment. I got something that looked like a decision: a single shoulder shrug with a half-head-turn chaser. The set was on sale—a big sale—and I was thrilled. It looked like we both would achieve our stated goals.

I was there. I had it: the perfect blend of style and savings. In the car on the way home, I did what men have not figured out how *not* to do for a thousand years: I talked. I said these words: "Hey, how about Costco?" What was I thinking? I couldn't stuff the words back in my mouth.

Once inside Costco, there it was. The perfect outdoor dining set for only $600 more than the one we had just left at the other store. All I had to do was shut up and drive home. But no, I had to speak. Four words: $150 per word.

Anybody need a 3-D Last Supper?

KATHY'S WAZOO

I used to blame my inability to grow plants on my urban upbringing, but Berneice grew up on a farm in Tennessee and can't grow anything either, so I can't blame concrete. It's a skill we don't possess. We love the idea of growing something—anything really—but we've reached the point where it seems unnecessarily cruel to bring a living thing into our home.

I wanted to leave my two lemon trees alone so they could do their business. I figured they'd have a better chance of pollinating if no one was watching.

Our friend Kathy Bye has lemons coming out the wazoo. She has a Meyer lemon tree, and it's prolific. I'm not sure she could stop the lemon production if she wanted to—they pop out like pimples on a teenager. She literally turns lemons into lemonade. She gives her homemade limoncello as gifts. Even her husband, Ray, smells lemony fresh.

This would be a good time to mention that I kill things. Houseplants, herbs, grass, trees, shrubs, bushes—if it grows, I can kill it in record time. My neighbor can confirm that the phrase "The grass is always greener on the other side" is not true; my lawn looks like a grenade-testing area. I failed to grow mulch.

If I even call a gardening store, they have four plants die. I stopped to admire a friend's rosebush, and it withered in a week. I was once given a fern as a gift, and I could hear it scream. I'm pretty sure I once killed an artificial ficus. Plants know I'm a death sentence. It's not about if—just when.

I planted an orange tree in my backyard ten years ago. The only thing it's produced is sharp spikes. Seriously, not one orange in a decade but thousands of spikes. Not only won't it give me any fruit, but it's armed itself. It mocks me.

The thing is I really want to be able to grow something. The concept of eating something I actually grew is pretty cool. I don't want to be on my deathbed realizing that the only thing I successfully grew was hair.

So when Kathy shared her lemon success, I thought maybe this is it. She said any idiot could grow a Meyer lemon tree. So I went online and was filled with hope when the ad said, "Any idiot can grow a Meyer lemon tree." Hey, I'm an idiot—I can do this.

Completely ignoring my black-thumb history, I planted a Meyer in the perfect sunny spot. Six months later, it gave me a lemon. One lemon. I nurtured that lemon. It was my new lemon baby. It started out the size of a grape, and for weeks it sputtered along. Soon it was a golf ball—go, lemon, go! It wasn't dying. What had I done right?

When it got about as big as a kitten's head, it stopped growing and started getting more yellow. I assumed this was good. Unable to contain my enthusiasm, I went out to the south forty (side of my house) and plucked the little jewel. It smelled like a lemon. It tasted like a lemon. I grew a lemon! I was finally a farmer.

That was three years ago, and it was also my last lemon. One stinking lemon, but the tree is still alive. I viewed my glass of lemonade as half-full, so I sought out professional help (not for me, for the tree). The diagnosis was that the tree needed to cross-pollinate. I had to get my tree a spouse.

After six months, there were no lemons on the old tree, but strangely the new tree sprouted two lemons—twins! It seems I also need help matchmaking, because the husband got pregnant.

That's two trees and almost four years to yield three lemons. I guess I could follow Kathy's lead and give them as gifts. I mean, who doesn't like a thimble of limoncello?

BEYOND LIQUID-PLUMR

It's amazing to me how frequently I catch myself doing stereo-typical male things. I honestly consider myself more enlight-ened. I guess that's how life works: we never quite grasp who we really are because the acceptance of that reality might be too much to handle.

It's really hard for a man to admit it's time to call a plumber, but she forced me to do it.

I remember the first time I saw her, sitting in the corner next to a rich-looking double vanity. Sleek, black, and with a gold handle, she was taller than most, but it was her elongated seat that caught my eye. She was everything I could have ever wanted in a toilet and more. She was the Beyoncé of toilets.

Little did I know, this was to be the relationship I regretted most in my life and the start of an eight-year battle of wills. To this day she mocks me.

If it's true that your instincts allow you to know about a relationship from the first flush, then I should have known.

She seemed off—like a sputtering engine not getting gas. But because I'm a man, her sheer beauty allowed me to overlook any obvious signs of a problem. Again and again, her flushes were irregular. They were never the same and never quite right. A powerless swirl, an awkward sideways sloshing, a burping double splash with a bubble, and even the dreaded fast-fill-up scare before a counterclockwise and quick empty. It's as if she had an endless bowl of tricks to keep me off balance.

It took a long time to call a plumber. It's like asking for directions: men just don't acknowledge failure very well. Satan could be coming out of the drain, and we're still pretty convinced we can fix it with a gallon of Liquid-Plumr and a wire thing you unwind into the drain hole. We are even more convinced that the first gallon of Liquid-Plumr almost got things moving, so we buy a second gallon. After spending a year and five times what a plumber would have cost, we quietly acknowledge that perhaps it would be a good time to call one. We mumble it to our wife while she's on the phone with her sister. When she asks what we said, we say, "Nothing," but technically we did tell her.

The first plumber I called walked into the bathroom and took one look at her and said, "She's a beauty." I felt my chest tighten, and I looked him square in the eye and said, "That is exactly how it started with me. Her handle may be gold, but her heart is coal."

"What's the problem?" he asked, with an innocence that could only have come from years of success. "The problem!?" I said, with a high voice and a flutter of my developing eye twitch. "She overflows, won't flush anything larger than a marble, makes obscene noises in the middle of the night, ruins dinner parties, makes children cry, and—I can't be 100 percent certain of this last one—I think about a month ago she flushed herself."

I left the bathroom as he prepared to dive in. Twenty minutes later he emerged, looking like he had wrestled a beaver in a gunnysack. He didn't say much and refused to make eye contact. With his head cocked in shame, he mouthed, "Sorry, no charge," as he hustled away.

I realized then that I didn't need a plumber—I needed an exorcist. I asked the best construction minds in town to tell me the plumber they would call if their life depended on their toilet. They whispered a name as though I had poked into a secret society. I should call the one known only as The Plunger.

I remember the day The Plunger showed up at my door: there was a soft light around him, a kind of heavenly glow. He had a tool belt with many shiny things—something that looked like a hook with a camera, a gun-looking thing with an air cylinder attached, and a pouch holding a spray can embossed with a skull and crossbones. I'm pretty sure he had all he needed to remove my kidney. Standing in front of me was the hired gunslinger of plumbers. He put his hand on my shoulder and said, "I've got this."

As I watched him walk to the bathroom, I noticed that even his plumber's butt had a stylish wink. I poured a drink and waited. I heard a clank and then a sort of whoosh. Silence, a splash followed by more silence. Then what sounded like two iron skillets banging together, a kind of fingernail-on-a-blackboard sound, and then what I would describe as the sound of a sack of wet laundry being dropped off a second-floor balcony.

He looked a little rough when he came out, but he had a confident strut. "All fixed. Good to go." Wow, he really was the toilet whisperer. He handed me a bill, and I knew not to insult him by looking at it. He tipped his hat and was gone—leaving only the slight whisper of ammonia in the air.

Twenty minutes after he was gone, I heard a gurgle and then a watery burp. Well played Beyoncé, well played.

UNFRIENDLY SKIES

The only problem I have with flying is that it takes place off the ground. Other than that, it's still pretty unpleasant.

Midway through my fear-of-flying therapy, I realized it wasn't flying I was afraid of. What freaked me out was plunging to my death in a cigar tube, sitting next to a big, sweaty guy from New Jersey.

I'll admit to having a few phobias. I don't like tall bridges, flying, heights, snakes, clowns, deep water, or small, confined spaces (think MRIs). I'm slightly troubled by spiders, movies with subtitles, bad waiters, and loud talkers, but I don't put those in the phobia category.

Slowly I am finding ways to cope with all these life interruptions. I've figured out how to deal with the MRI issue. It had gotten pretty bad. I felt like I was being loaded into a torpedo tube. Despite my brain telling me it was a medical procedure, my gut told me there was a guy looking through a periscope searching for a target. Even with enough Valium to stop a panther, I was still able to last only a few minutes. A smart technician put a washcloth over my eyes so I could open them without seeing where I was, and it worked. Remember that one, future MRIers.

I try and work around the other phobias, so unless I'm trapped in a tiny car with clowns going over a tall bridge on the way to an airport, I can usually manage things. If we absolutely have to drive over a tall bridge, Berneice gets behind the wheel. In Delaware, home of a ridiculously high bridge, they actually have folks who you can pay to drive your car across—pretty much the only good reason to live in Delaware. Apparently, you hand the drive-over guy the key and then go fetal on the floorboard.

I once got caught in the wrong lane and had to go over Tampa's Sunshine Skyway Bridge—at night, in a cloud. Technically it was fog, but when you are high enough to have to dodge the Pearly Gates, then it's a cloud. I could only see ten feet in front of the car, but I knew how high I was, which made it worse. I realized that you don't need a near-death experience to see heaven—it was about twenty feet to my right. For a moment I thought I saw Gandhi in my backseat, but I realized later it was just a towel and a batting helmet.

It gets worse. If you've ever driven the Skyway Bridge, you know it exits onto a roundabout off-ramp, which in the cloud quickly blends into the on-ramp heading back onto the bridge. My worst nightmare times two.

I made it, but I was five pounds lighter, and it took a spatula to pry my fingers off the steering wheel.

In the last two weeks, I've had two good friends talk to me about their extreme fear of flying, and I'm guessing there are a lot more of us out there, so I wanted to share my successful therapy experience.

I was a ritual flyer. If I had to get on a plane, I needed every bit of good juju I could carry. My Xanax-induced stash included my lucky gold watch, a portable DVD player (little known fact:

if you don't make eye contact with the Grim Reaper, he'll move to the people in the exit row), and cherry cough drops (I had not been in a plane crash while sucking cherry cough drops, so they were essential).

I've never really had anything go wrong on a flight. I've been through some storms and had some bumps—but never one of those experiences that cause folks to swear off the friendly skies. The worst storm I was ever in was okay because I was sitting next to Rabbi Garfein and figured he was connected.

My problem was that I would have overwhelming panic attacks. Apparently, if you've never had a near-death experience on a plane (other than the food), your therapeutic prescription is different. One regimen is to take a few flights with your therapist so they can experience your trigger points and work you through the moment. At least that's what I was told. I never got that far.

I quickly realized that my health insurance didn't cover the series of flights my new near-death buddy and I would be taking together. After calculating five round-trip tickets for two and realizing that it would be cheaper to relocate my relatives to Florida, I went for the reduced-rate half cure: learning to deal with the panic attacks.

This is where the therapy got pretty cool. My psychologist asked me a remarkably simple question: Do I believe the panic attacks can kill me? I really had never thought of them in those terms. Anyone who's had panic attacks knows you feel like they're going to kill you, but they never do. Deep down, through the tight chest, sweaty palms, rapid breathing, and graying light of a panic attack, you know you're not dying. It may be eight minutes of hell, but it's not death.

So after I answered in the negative, he told me to just invite it when I feel one coming on. Tell my panic attack, "Come get me. I know you're not going to kill me, so let's just get it over with. Give me your best shot; I'm ready to freak out. Let's get on with it, because I have things to do when it's over. So bring it on, panic boy!"

Look, I'm not a doctor, although I do occasionally wear rubber gloves. I'm only telling you what worked for me. I haven't had another panic attack, and today I fly without any problems—other than sitting next to the big, sweaty guy from New Jersey. So you might want to give it a try. If it doesn't work, I've got a DVD player and a package of cherry cough drops you can have.

I'm keeping the gold watch, just in case.

MOM'S NEWFANGLED PHONE

My mother is not afraid of new technology—it's the other way around. I have become convinced that her pure will as a powerful Jewish Mother can actually alter the physical universe—something Siri learned the hard way.

My ninety-one-year-old father sent me a text message with a photo of his new socks. They were on his feet. I stared at my phone for a minute, trying to decide how to respond. While I was musing about why I had just received a sock picture, I felt a sense of accomplishment: the text was a major victory in my continuing battle to teach my parents how to use their smartphones.

Life was simpler in the olden days (six months ago) when my parents had flip phones. No voice-prompting, picture-sending, face-timing foolishness. Make a call, answer a call. End of story. But now everything has changed.

I'm guessing that years ago I really upset a guy. Maybe I cut him off in traffic or was in front of him with eleven items in the

ten-items-or-less line. Whatever it was, it was enough for him
to quit his job, move to Daytona Beach, and start a career with
AT&T so he could get revenge years later by convincing my
parents to buy smartphones. I can't think of another reason for
that level of cruelty.

But hold on to your smart button! It turns out that Dad
sent me the sock picture because one sock had an *L* and the
other an *R*. I took solace in the fact that he wasn't just sending
me random pictures. (Now I feared that he had figured out
the ease of texting, he was going to start sending me a series
of themed clothing shots, and from there it's a slippery slope
to pictures of his TV remote, car keys, and toothbrush.) I was
wrong: Dad was using the phone feature as intended. I had
never seen directions on socks. It was a novelty. Well done,
Pops.

The technology has not come as easily to my eighty-nine-
year-old Jewish mother. I developed a nasty purple welt on my
forehead from banging it on a table while trying to teach her to
use the iPhone voice prompt, Siri.

Me: *This is simple, Mom. You just hold down this button,
and when you hear the beep, you say what you want the phone
to do.*

Mom: (pushing the button and hearing the beep) *Now?*

Siri: *Now what?*

Me: *You have to say what you want as soon as you hear the
beep.*

Mom: (pushing the button again and hearing the beep)
Talk now?

Siri: *I don't really talk much, as electronic speech is trig-
gered by user interaction.*

Mom: *What did she say?*

Me: (rubbing my forehead) *Mom, she is just answering
what you asked.*

Mom: *I'm not even talking to her.*

Me: *I know. But she knows to start when she hears the beep, so let's try this again.*

Mom: (pushing the button, and upon hearing the beep yells into the phone like someone was holding it in another state): *CAN I SEND A MESSAGE TO MY SON?*

Siri: *I don't know who your child is, and—in fact—I don't know who you are.*

Mom: (now using this as a teaching moment for Siri, speaks into the phone) *That's not very nice.*

Me: *It's not personal, Mom. You don't need to ask permission.*

Mom: *Who cares about permission? She doesn't even know me, and already she's giving me attitude.*

Me: *Let's try this again, but this time only say what you want her to do.*

Mom pushes the button, hears the beep, and now looks at me while silently mouthing, "Now?"

I tilt my head, looking like a confused puppy, and before I can stop myself, I actually say out loud, "Yes, talk now."

Siri: *What do you want me to say?*

Mom: *She's an idiot.*

Me: (banging my head on the table) *Good Lord!*

Siri: *I found twenty-three churches near you.*

STOCKED CARS AND TOW TRUCKS

My writing mentor, Mary Ann Lindley, told me early on that good writers go through life like a shark and take a bite out of everything. This next adventure was a very big bite.

Once our car finally skidded to a stop, it didn't take long for us to realize that civilization as we know it ceases to exist twenty-two feet from the edge of the Interstate 10 asphalt.

If you're ever going to be stranded in a remote area with only a car for shelter, you're going to want it to be my car. I admit, much to my wife's amusement, I stock my car like it's a bomb shelter on wheels. Before I get to our near tragedy on Interstate 10, I'll share just a few of the items I keep in my car—or what Berneice calls my "List of Dysfunction," just in case some of you guys need some tips on what your cars are missing.

Machete (should be obvious)

Glow sticks (just because they're cool)

String and rope (because they do different things)

Duct tape (because as a man I'm required to have it with me at all times)

Bottled water (in case we are stranded in a desert)

Change of warm clothes and change of cool clothes (stranded in New Mexico or stranded in Canada)

Aspirin (had a friend have a heart attack in a car)

Bug spray (could get stranded in a swamp)

Small waterproof pouch (protecting phone if I need to walk through a swamp)

The thing that breaks windows (in case I plunge into a lake)

Flashlight (part of the window-breaking thing, just in case I plunge into a lake at night)

Small solar charger (charges phone if stranded in daylight)

Umbrellas (plural because for some unknown reason I have five of them)

Small folding shovel (technically to dig out a tire stuck in sand, but actually I saw it in Bass Pro Shops for $6 and couldn't pass it up)

Two sets of jumper cables (don't ask)

A $20 bill (in case I'm stranded close enough for $20 to get me home)

Protein bars (to survive until found by a helicopter)

Plastic knife and fork set (in case friends drop by the stranded site for dinner)

A plastic bag with a postage stamp (This one even stumped me. I'm guessing I put it there in case I need to send a letter to get help.)

So, we were traveling on Interstate 10 about five miles from nowhere. The car was loaded with all we would need to visit family on Florida's east coast. As usual, we had grossly over-packed—bikes, beach umbrellas, coolers, literally five containers of baked goods, and our living room sectional. Picture the Griswolds.

While generally going the legal speed limit, the car shut off. The steering wheel locked up, and all I could do was drift off the shoulder and find a small patch of shade. The first thing I did was pop open the hood. I may as well have opened a bag of cookies. There are things under the hood of a car—hot things—beyond my scope of understanding. It occurred to me that a better use of my time would be to call AAA. You would think waiting for a tow truck on a Sunday on Interstate 10 just outside of Nowheresville would be rough, but it was the recognition that we had inadvertently driven into the jungle that freaked us out.

We travel these highways every day and watch the landscape as we whiz by, but let me tell you that twenty-two feet off the interstate is a different planet. We soon saw mosquitos so big they had landing gear. An army of gnats quickly organized into an attack force and filled our car. My bug spray may as well have been Kool-Aid. Berneice stepped out of the car, and a snake slithered across her foot. I fully expected to be hit by a blow dart.

Has this other world always been there, mere feet off the asphalt? All my emergency equipment was useless. This was the one contingency I had never planned for: the Amazon scenario. It was only a matter of time until this infested labyrinth consumed us. They would find us bloodless, clutching glow sticks and umbrellas.

Mercifully, Mike the tow truck guy finally showed up. He was at ease in this new world, which explained his lack of concern about the large spider on his shoulder. "What seems to be the problem?" he asked. "Well, the car just shut off, and I managed to pull off the highway. There's a family of hornets in my cup holder, and I'm pretty sure I'm in the first stages of malaria."

In between spitting, Mike said, "Well, let's get you folks loaded up and see if we can't get you someplace where they can fix this car." My face lit up with hope. "Wow, you think there's a place open today?" Mike snickered. "Oh, yeah, there's a few places open today, just none that fix cars." You gotta love country humor.

He loaded us up and towed us to J & W Auto Repair, a small shop near Live Oak, Florida, which may or may not open on Monday, depending on J's or W's mood. We saw a Jiffy Mart just up the road. My chest swelled with pride. We had missed lunch, so that $20 bill was going to come in real handy.

And that, my friends, is why you stock your car.

ADULTS UNDER SIEGE

I've looked at the universe a bit differently ever since I started writing. Sometimes you know when an event will turn into a column. There was no doubt with this one. Seeing those poor forgotten parents, I knew this one was bound to be a classic.

The children's play area in the Saint Louis Galleria mall is carefully designed: walled in by four-foot-high barriers with a gated opening and a forest of glossy molded structures to climb on and through. A mushroom. A big cat. A caterpillar tunnel and more. Fifteen happy little kids running and climbing. This would be the place to sit and catch my breath after being worn out by our grandson, an adorable tornado named Luke.

We have three grandchildren in our blended family and another on the way: Luke in Missouri, Rachel and Leonardo in Maine. Three and a half perfectly perfect kids. (Would you expect anything less?)

On this fateful morning, Luke's parents handed over a perfectly happy child at 7:35 a.m. The first ten minutes were joyful and without incident. By 7:50 a.m. I saw the first sign of a frown and the inevitable collapse. Let the walking, patting, pacifier holding, bottle tilting, passing back and forth, stuffed-animal fake voicing, high-pitched baby talking, and battery-operated mobile twirling begin. By 8:06 a.m., the *Titanic* had hit the iceberg. We were fresh out of tricks, and Luke knew it. Time to try a surefire old trick: let's get this kid in the car and head to the nearest mall. If the drive doesn't do it, the walk will.

We arrive at the mall, and the sound of children laughing was like a beacon showing us the way to the children's playscape. We'll just sit like a couple of sponges and soak up the joy. Above the din of the children, I couldn't help but notice the parents. My concern grew as I scanned the faces one by one. They looked like a group of plane crash survivors—alive but dazed.

One dad looked like he had been hit in the back of the head by a sack of pacifiers: unscarred but confused. One mom had her hair sticking straight out to the side like someone had put a blow-dryer in her other ear. Another had a dollop of something green over her eyebrow. I continued to peruse the gallery. A woman was squeezing a juice box onto her shoe without realizing it. Another was bobbing her head in an effort to stay awake. A dad peered over the wall, as if he were looking for a way out. Another mom had crayon streaks on her thigh, as if she'd been marked for sacrifice. Things were getting clearer.

One kid ran up and kicked his dad in the shin. I surmised that he was sent as a scout to test the perimeter. At first I thought Luke was just thinking he would like to be out there—only in time did I begin to suspect he might be giving in to some ancient ritual, like a new recruit learning how to pack his footlocker.

Out of the molded cat's mouth, a knee-high leader appeared, as if he had been coughed up like a hairball. With a rubber sword in hand, his seemingly random movements were now forming a strategic pattern. The other children continued to play, but even their movements were settling into a cadence. I could see it now: it was time to get out before the gate was blocked. I abandoned the "No parent left behind" pledge and took off.

I'll never know what happened to that group of parenting victims. Maybe they all made it home safely, or maybe this wasn't the day scheduled for the siege.

An African proverb opines that with each generation you learn to love deeper. Loosely translated, it suggests that your children are love practice, that by the time you get to your grandchildren, you understand love in a more profound way.

Perhaps it's that by then we've learned to unpack the heart baggage we gathered as young parents. Now, uncluttered by the responsibility of raising these third-generation little folks, we see the simple truth in them. I know that each time they look at me and smile, I'm stabbed in the heart. Not that their parents have offered, but I'd buy a ticket just to watch them sleep. At least it's safe when they're sleeping.

OBITS

The older I get the more I read the obituaries while looking out of the corner of my eye with my head tilted to the side. Kind of like driving past a car accident: I can't help but look, but I really don't want to. The frequency of seeing people I know is not fun. But the cold, distant information I consistently see in obits got me thinking.

I imagine a doctor bursting through the doors, yelling, "We've figured out a way to grow a whole person from just a finger!" And my wife looking at our children and saying, "Wow, your dad was right—go figure."

As a high-functioning hypochondriac, I feel a responsibility to think about death with some frequency. I admire people who are reconciled about their passing. I have good friends who have shared their personal peace with the inevitable. I'm jealous of the calm they feel when they embrace their mortality. Not so much for me. I'm terrified of not being here and have every intention of fighting off death as long as possible. Not to overstate it, but even the possibility of a dark eternal void of nothingness is at best a little troubling.

I wonder what it would be like to never see the Cubs win a World Series in my lifetime. And, oh yeah, not seeing my grandchildren.

I've left my family specific instructions to never pull the plug. If, after being hit by a bus, all that's left of me is a finger, I would like it kept alive. I'll be just fine communicating by pointing at things until medical science figures out a way to attach the rest of a body to a living finger.

I'm not totally consumed with death, although I admit it's exhausting trying to fight it off each day. I'm the only entirely healthy person I know who looks at fireworks on the Fourth of July and hopes it's not the last time I'll see them. While I would love to just give in to the spectacular sky show, I think it's only prudent to consider the dark possibility. It's like that for most holidays. Nothing takes the starch out of Thanksgiving dinner like wondering if it's your last meal.

I consider myself a spiritual person, but reconciling the permanence of death is still elusive for me. I know there will be people of faith who will read this and want me to know that it will all be fine and that there's a better place. Maybe—but I'm just fine with my living room, and frankly I'd like to stay there as long as possible.

I'm guessing some of it is seeing a significant rise in people I know showing up in the obituaries. Actually, I'm strangely drawn to the obits. It troubles me that someone's life is summed up in just a few paragraphs with a small black-and-white photo. It seems like such a missed opportunity. I say go out swinging and write your own obituary now, before you're just a finger.

Just get it written and stick it in a file. And don't be burdened by actual facts. This is your last chance to leave a good impression. Juice it up a little.

Put a few things in there that folks would have a hard time refuting. Accomplishments that even a Google search would fail to disprove, like you invented cashew butter or earwax remover. You paddled the Amazon River on a sofa cushion. You once made out with Golda Meir. Use asterisks to keep your conscience clean. You BASE jumped off the Empire State Building* and wrote the screenplay for *A Few Good Men*.**

Look, I've recently accepted that I'm probably not the only guy who gets to live forever, but for a death-phobe like me, the daily grind of worrying about dying is time well spent. Drop me a note. I'm available to help with obituary writing—just don't wait too long. It will take forever with just one finger.

Actually, took the elevator

**Actually, just saw the movie*

HAMMERHEAD

If you've ever attempted a home project more complicated than screwing in a lightbulb or tried to figure out the hiero- glyphics called directions, then you'll understand this one.

I knew a guy who worked at a sawmill for twenty-five years. He has two and a half fingers left. I totally get it.

It's not that I'm not allowed to do home repair projects, but let's just say the practice is frowned upon. There have been a series of unfortunate incidents over the years, which may have been at least partially related to my skills as a handyman. The larger problem could be my lack of patience when it comes to reading directions.

To me, directions are not gospel; they are more of a sug- gestion. Printed project directions are really some passive-ag- gressive person's idea of punishing us. You finish a project, and there are always two screws, a bolt, and three washers left over. That's not a big deal if you're building a birdhouse, but it's pretty freaky if you just finished an inversion table. On the bright side, it became my own private inversion table because no one else had the courage to lead with their head on a piece of equipment built by me.

While the rest of the world is using laser printers, the guys who print directions are using Etch A Sketches. They're always blurry, every screw looks the same, and there is no visible difference between a number three wooden dowel and a number seven thumb bolt—they both look like a smudge. You get the feeling that two guys are alone in some warehouse in Des Moines high-fiving each other because they have designed another page of unreadable directions.

The only power tool I own is a hand drill. I actually did own a chainsaw for exactly one slice. A tree had come down in our yard, and I fired it up, took one good push into the tree, and it jammed. I couldn't get it out. Just as I was putting both feet on the tree for leverage and getting ready to pull, I got a quick image of my ear ending up in my neighbor's yard and shut the project down.

I have eighty-seven screwdrivers and forty-nine pliers, because like most men I can't resist when the hardware store bundles a set of ten and teasingly puts them next to the register on the way out. I'm sure there will be at least one in the set I don't have, and I know I'll need it one day. I have enough Allen wrenches to take apart the space shuttle, but if I see a cool new set, I'm all over it.

And here is the one inexorable truth about socket wrenches. (I just had to stop typing and ask a friend what you called the thing with a handle and round things that you put over bolts.) No matter how many socket sizes you have, you will come across a bolt they don't fit. Count on it.

I have had a few home projects go sour. Okay, more than a few—okay, a lot. Here are just two in the Yordon–Cox Failed Home Projects Hall of Fame:

The Ceiling Fan

As God is my witness, I thought that turning off the wall switch cut the power to the fan—if I designed houses, that's how I would do it. The idea of a breaker box never really occurred to me.

I was replacing the light thing that was attached to the fan over our bed. Because I'm a classic multitasker, I had my phone cradled on my shoulder while talking to my friend Kris as I performed the bulbectomy. I only share that because Kris has actually been on the audio end of a few of my home disasters. A few months earlier I was talking to her when I tried to nail a bat house to a tree while standing on a sixteen-foot ladder perched on a slope. That project was eleven seconds of failure.

Everything was going well with the fan project until I pinched together what I thought were two dead wires. I vaguely remember a flash of light as I was launched off the bed into our walk-in closet. I remember the smell of burning hair and seeing a wisp of smoke while lying on my back. I was a five-foot-ten human sparkler. It took a minute to uncross my eyes, and I had to ask my aunt Mary (who had died twenty years earlier) to leave the closet.

Lesson learned: put pillows on floor of closet.

The Wagner Power Painter

I wanted to surprise Berneice by painting our family room while she was out. As usual, I wanted to complete the project with minimal effort, so the power painter was the way to go. I gave the room my usual level of preparation by shoving furniture and everything else to the middle of the room. There was certainly no reason to cover anything.

It's simple: The power painter is filled with paint, then strapped to your back like a scuba diver's air tank. You flick the switch, point the handle, and start spraying the walls. At least that's the theory. Remember I mentioned that whole "read the directions" thing? They *may* have mentioned not to use oil-based paint because it will clog the unit.

So the motor is running, and I'm pointing the spray handle at the walls, but nothing is coming out. What I don't know is that the tank on my back is swelling up like a giant paint-filled tick.

You know that moment of blissful unawareness when you sense something is happening but you're not sure what it is? I turned to look, but the giant tick turned with me, still out of my sight line, right up until it burst. The only place there wasn't paint was the walls. Everything I had stacked uncovered in the middle of the room was now a soft shade of beige. I had also been painted. Stunned, I rushed to the garage and scrubbed myself with paint thinner.

I was gone when Berneice got home. She surveyed the carnage and was able to reach me at the ER, where I was being treated for burns caused by paint thinner.

Lesson learned: strap paint tank to chest so I can see it expanding.

I know my friend from the sawmill would tell me not to let a few disasters get in the way of charging into my next project. He would stick one of his nubs in my chest and chide me to never give up. Then raise his hand and give me a high-two-and-a-half.

BLUEBERRY PANCAKES

Beyond everything else I hope to accomplish during my time on this planet, there are few things I hold sacred as much as being a good father. Even if I screw up everything else, I hope I got that one right.

In the river behind my parents' Daytona Beach home, there's an artificial reef made entirely of blueberry pancakes.

My father always got up early on Sunday mornings and got busy in the kitchen. By the time my three brothers and I stumbled downstairs, the giant stack of pancakes had already been layered. Holding his spatula like a scepter, he would proclaim, "The world is like a mirror reflecting what you do—when you smile at it, it smiles right back at you."

Seriously. He said that every single time.

Dad making blueberry pancakes was as regular as the sunrise, and over the years I've come to understand the importance of the ritual, even if the actual pancakes were tough to choke down. I never had the heart to tell my dad I didn't like his pancakes, because he got such a thrill making them. So I always slipped out and fed the fish.

Everything I know about optimism I got from Dad. He's a lifelong Chicago Cubs fan. In his ninety-one years, the team has never won a World Series, but each spring he's convinced to his core that this will be the year. There's never been a February when I didn't hear "I really like this team. I have a good feeling about this year." His baseball heart is broken every summer, but by the next spring, he's nine years old and full of hope.

Recently he was taken by ambulance and rushed into emergency surgery for a bleeding ulcer. When I finally was able to talk to him just hours after his surgery, I nervously asked how he was feeling. "Great" was his response because "great" is always his response. If he had a railroad spike in his head, he would say, "Look, son, another place to hang my shirts." His life glass is always half-full.

Optimism was just one layer of the real lesson my father taught me. The real lesson was that being a good father was job one. Everything else in life fell in line after that. You would need a calculator to count the parenting mistakes I've made, so I think we can eliminate "World's Best Dad" from any of my future T-shirts, but I'm pretty comfortable knowing my dad's most valuable lesson was learned. Nothing is more important to me than my boys, and it fills my heart to know they know that.

I've never met Steve Hart, but I'd like to. I saw on Facebook how he drove across town on a Tuesday morning to pick up Darius, his five-year-old boy, from school. He made the trip because a tractor was going to be digging a big hole in their backyard for a pool, and he didn't want the boy to miss the big dig. For a five-year-old boy, a tractor digging a hole is as good as it gets. Steve wasn't going to make the evening news, but it was a pretty cool dad move.

In 1894 on a green field in Tallahassee, Florida, David Hanselman's great-grandfather shot a deer with his Marlin rifle. Last fall, on a green field in Tallahassee, David's son Trevor shot his first deer with his great-great-grandfather's Marlin rifle. David understood the importance of sewing together the fabric of time and knew that one day Trevor would understand the depth of what his father had done. Connecting his son with his great-great-grandfather was a pretty good dad thing to do.

I've come to understand that being a great dad isn't about doing great things but a collection of a thousand good ones, like making sure a tractor digging a hole isn't missed or dusting off an old rifle.

Or maybe just waking up early to make blueberry pancakes.

A CHRISTMAS MIRACLE

If I had a big lump of coal that day, I know exactly where I would have shoved it.

Now, Sneezer! Now, Hacker!
Now, Prayer and Sweater!
On, Stripper! On, Screamer!
Now fly away! Fly away!
Fly away all!

It was right after Christmas, and the 6:15 p.m. Delta out of Atlanta to Tallahassee, Florida, was delayed. Not just bad weather—*really* bad weather. But in case you're not familiar with that flight, it can be delayed because the pilot has the wrong socks. It doesn't take much. It's a small jet: fourteen rows with two seats on each side. Like a flying pastry bag full of people instead of icing. Sardines would think it was small.

The flight starts with the pilot announcing that the air-conditioning is out and some of the cabin lights are not working—and "Oh, by the way, thanks for choosing Delta!"

We sat on the tarmac for about thirty minutes while other planes landed. Finally, the pilot announced we had to wait because of the weather. Other planes circling the airport were running low on fuel and needed to get on the ground. I looked around for Bonnie Bedelia.

Finally, it was our turn to take off. I'm . . . thrilled? Look, I'm fine with flights that have occasional bumps of rough air. But this flight had the occasional smooth—a virtual bounce house from the time we took off until we landed. It was like flying inside a mechanical bull. I've had more pleasant experiences in an MRI.

The passengers were melting in the muggy heat. The air was stifling, and our nervous silence was broken by a woman across the aisle having a sneezing fit. She started with a run of five consecutive and finished with eight more at ten-second intervals. Not petite little dainty sneezes, but ones that were shot out of a '77 Camaro exhaust pipe. Up one row from her was the cougher. She was relentless and hacking like a lumberjack. Everyone on the plane wanted to reach in and clear her throat, but unbuckling your seat belt was a huge risk. I would have offered her a cough drop, but it sounded like she needed a plunger. Whatever bugs those two had were now our new, unwrapped Christmas presents.

Passengers were peeling off clothes like Vegas strippers. I put a five-dollar bill in the waistband of the woman behind me—she was down to tights and a sports bra. The guy next to me was using the emergency instruction sheet as a fan. I would have screamed "Mommy," but some guy a few rows up had already used that line. I thought about trying to make my way to the bathroom but quickly realized that if I made it there I would be in a flying blender.

The flight attendant emerged from the darkness with a bottle of water and some plastic cups. He offered water, but what we really needed was an IV cart or, at the very least, a priest.

Finally, in his one merciful act, the pilot said the magic words "In preparation for landing, please stow away any personal items you may have been using." Since my personal items were scattered over seven rows, I decided to just sit back and pray. I thought the pilot had traded places with the baggage handler. He bounced the plane off the runway like he was skipping stones.

So thanks, Delta, for a rip-roaring Christmas gift. Next flight, we can save some time. I'll buy the ticket, and instead of getting on the plane, I'll just come to the airport and you can smack me around with a sack of hammers.

BRIDGE VIEWS

I find myself writing more frequently about where I live. I take pride in my hometown. But this column is really more about where any of us live and the importance of not looking past what's right in front of us.

It was a chilly Friday evening the week before Christmas. I was halfway across a small bridge in the sleepy waterfront town of Carrabelle, Florida, when I looked over my left shoulder. What I saw confirmed that for me a decision I had made forty-one years ago to call North Florida home was the right one. Hang on to that thought.

The Grey Dog is a hole-in-the-wall breakfast place in Greenwich Village. You walk in and run smack into a wall of breakfast aroma: muffins, bagels, and coffee, all mixed together. A couple of wobbly tables, a waiter with a T-shirt emblazoned with "Let's eat Grandma. Let's eat, Grandma. Commas save lives."

One entire wall is brick. Not a fancy new brick because some designer thought it would look cool—but because it was the wall from the building next door someone built ninety years ago. There's a familiar din—locals doing nothing but being locals.

Berneice and I had found exactly what we were looking for: a cool little New York breakfast place. The pancake was great, but not better than the ridiculous maple-schmeared pancake at Bada Bean, the small Tallahassee boutique diner. Everything we ordered came with a side of New York, and that's just what we were looking for. We loved it, but it wasn't better than the coffee and conversations we have with Mike, the owner of The Egg Café & Eatery in Tallahassee, another of our favorite breakfast stops.

When you come out of the mountains in Spain and head to Málaga, the anticipation of seeing the Mediterranean is pretty cool. Actually, the last mile before that first view is through an older industrial section, and the first look at the Mediterranean is past a less-than-inspiring roadside park. But the mystique of the old sea was real, and we jumped out to capture the moment in pictures.

I promise you, if I put aside the romance of the moment, the view was not prettier than the first moment you turn the corner just past Panacea, Florida, and see the Gulf of Mexico on Highway 98. The view isn't older than the Gulf, but somehow the sense of Mediterranean history overwhelms you.

Tell the story at your next dinner party about turning the corner and seeing the Mediterranean, and everyone will give an audible sigh. Tell them about turning the corner on Highway 98 and seeing the Gulf, and someone will ask you to pass the salt. I get it.

I understand the importance of getting away. Sometimes you just need to change the view, see new things, taste new food. But what's changed for me is a new appreciation of what's around me every day. It doesn't mean I don't want to see new things; it's just given me a chance to really see. I mean *really see* what's been right in front of me all along.

My friend David Hanselman has a home on Live Oak Island, Florida, and he gets lost in his love for that place when he talks of its allure. "It's where life transitions," he tells me, "from the woods, to the marshes, to the sea. All seen in one view."

David has not missed what's right in front of him.

And it's more than just places—it's people. I just had a cab driver in DC ranting about the state of the union. I listened, but my focus wasn't so much on the content as it was on the Capraesque moment of getting to hear the wisdom of a cab driver in DC.

But spend thirty minutes at a Kiwanis Club of Tallahassee Northside meeting with four crusty older guys pontificating about city hall, and you realize what charmed you about the cab in DC was right in front of you, in your town.

You don't need to go to Williamsport to see an American tradition. Go sit at a local Little League game at Myers Park and just enjoy the show. The parents, the kids playing, and the kids not playing—all of it. There will be fifty things to make you smile.

Sometimes what's right in front of you is the hardest thing to see. Maybe it's because we are just used to looking at it. It takes a conscious effort to look at things you've seen a thousand times and see them as new and appreciate them for what they are. And I think that's true for people as well.

When you add a layer of "someplace else" over anything, it can seem more interesting. What I saw over my left shoulder that December evening in Carrabelle was kind of a marriage of lights. The docked fishing boats and the small town's Christmas lights all blending together. If you had sent me a postcard from Cape Cod with that picture, I would have sighed and thought how much I would love to be there to see it—and then I realized I already was.

DAD'S RECLINER

Sometimes the things I write make me laugh. I'll be sitting at my computer and catch myself laughing out loud at what I'm writing. This was one of those pieces. I was hearing my mom's voice the entire time.

About five minutes into hearing my eighty-eight-year-old Jewish mother answering my simple question, I put down the phone and made a sandwich. When I picked up the phone again, she hadn't skipped a beat.

It was an innocent question. My parents had been looking for a new recliner for my father. The search lasted for weeks and had finally ended with a bargain. All was right with the world. In a momentary lapse of judgment, I asked Mom a simple question:

Does Dad like the chair? Three . . . two . . . one . . . liftoff.

"We went to the Sears Outlet. That's not the store . . . it's the outlet. The prices are better. We tried Sam's, but your father didn't like their chairs, they were too hard. So we went to Sears—the outlet Sears. They had one for $169. No, wait. It was $170—I think about $181 with tax. But they wanted to charge $85 to deliver it, and I said no way. So when we go back, they'll put it in the car for $20, and when we get home our friend Bob can bring it in. It was originally $450. No, wait, $470. So it was a great deal. It's a new kind of fabric, not leather. I can't remember what you call the fabric—not velvet, but soft. LENNY, what's the name of the fabric on the chair? LENNY!! He can't hear me. It's soft, like velvet, but it's not velvet. We had crab legs last night for dinner. We got them at Sam's. You can freeze them and have them anytime you want. They were delicious. It's not denim, but it's soft. LENNY, WHAT WAS THE FABRIC ON THE CHAIR!?!? He can't hear me. We were on that side of town for something else, and I told your father we should just go into the Sears Outlet and see if they have a chair. What could we lose by just looking? You know at our age it doesn't need to last that long."

This is where I put the phone down and made a sandwich and then took a moment to fill the cat's water bowl. Thumbed through a couple of pieces of mail and then picked up the phone. Mom was still in perfect rhythm.

"You know I would have never thought about getting seafood from Sam's, but I thought why not. The fish don't know it's Sam's. They're fish. And by the way your father's blood sugar is 104—that's almost perfect. He tried a bunch of chairs. I mean Sam's has good crab legs, but their chairs, not so good. Your father doesn't need leather, he just wants it to be soft, you know, not hard. So when the Sears guy told me $85, I'm thinking we can fit this chair in the car. If not, I guess they can deliver it. But that's $181 plus $85. I mean who charges $85 to deliver a $181 chair? That's nuts! And let me tell you, Bob can move things. If it can be moved, Bob can move it. LENNY, WHAT'S THE NAME OF THE FABRIC!?!? *(ten-second pause)* Your father says it's soft. I TOLD HIM IT WAS SOFT . . . WHAT'S THE FABRIC CALLED? *(ten-second pause)* He says it's not leather. You know we usually get our seafood from Publix, but after these crab legs, I'm thinking maybe Sam's has some decent fish. You can get almost anything from Sam's except a soft chair. But I think Sam's delivers for free, but then you're stuck with a hard chair, and I start thinking maybe your father's butt is worth $85. How are the kids?"

Mom, does Dad like the chair?

FLU SHOTS AND TURKEY MELTS

This one really bothered me. I wanted to write it for a long time and finally got it off my chest. I try not to use my space to preach, mostly because I've got my own sock full of dysfunction, but it's troubling to have companies balancing their books on the backs of those in need. We can do better.

It was the Subway at exit 387 near Gainesville, Florida. Across the counter full of cut veggies and processed meat stood a skinny teenage boy with a paper hat. I looked him in the eye and held up a picture of the Subway Turkey Italiano Melt I had cut out of a magazine and told him I wanted my sandwich to look like the picture. There was an awkward pause, and then we both burst out laughing at the same time.

I'm not a big fan of fast food, but I understand. If Subway—or for that matter any fast-food joint—actually gave us products that looked like their advertising, they wouldn't be fast. But if we're willing to order our food over a speaker and get it in a sack, then it's best we keep our expectations low.

Lately, there's been a shift in corporate advertising that seems to count on us not paying attention, or maybe they think we can't handle truth. Like the attorney who says he's there for us in case we have an accident, even though the small print at the end of his ad says he's not licensed to practice in your state. If you live here, you get some lawyer who's not in the commercial.

Or the cable company whose TV ad has a young couple asking if the company has all the channels they like. The company spokesman says, "We do have all the channels I like." Hello? It's so fast you hardly notice he absolutely failed to answer the question they asked, but you feel pretty good about someone getting the channels they like, even if it's not the customer.

These techniques aren't new—they're just unnecessarily deceiving, the product of some clever ad gurus thinking we'll never notice, and for the most part, they're right.

However, there's a recent trend in corporate advertising that is more troubling: companies pumping up their brand by using the less fortunate or the medically challenged to entice us, their customers, and to absolve their corporate conscience by opening our wallets. It's brilliant: the business gets to make the donation and gets a tax write-off, and we pay for it. We are actually paying them to enhance their image. You've seen it, but maybe you haven't stopped to consider what's happening.

Here's one. Walgreens ran a flu-shot promotion: "Get a shot. Give a shot." You pay for your flu shot, and they give one to "a child in need." Here's a thought, Walgreens: if there are kids who can't get a much-needed lifesaving shot, how about dipping into your corporate war chest and donating them yourself. Are you really telling us that if we don't show up for a shot, then a kid somewhere goes without one? Why does your interest in helping kids require our participation? If you have the means and there are kids who need the shot, then make it happen. Don't make a kid wait for us to come through your door. The flu isn't waiting—and neither should you.

When I decide to make a charitable contribution, I don't have a yard sale and tell folks that I'll take a buck off the top for the homeless shelter if you buy my toaster. If I believe in what the homeless shelter is doing, I send a check—I don't hold the shelter hostage until I sell my toaster.

There are organizations in every community who depend on people who have the means to help. It's a responsibility we all share. Our willingness to give to the less fortunate or to spend our money on finding a cure for some disease is what helps define our community character. Making us get a shot so folks can get the help they need shouldn't be part of the equation. Think about that next time a business tells you they'll help if you buy what they're selling.

I'm okay getting a Turkey Italiano Melt that doesn't look anything like the picture in a magazine, but I think twice about a business that chooses to help people only if they can sell me something.

RULES FROM THE *HOW TO BE A MAN* HANDBOOK

*I've written about roller-coaster versus merry-go-round rela-
tionships. It's not even a close call for me—the roller coaster is
my preferred option. There's nothing merry-go-round about
my wife, Berneice. Delightfully unpredictable is the best way
to describe what it's like when you visit our amusement park,
as I was reminded on this uncomfortable ride.*

It was a perfect Saturday. Berneice and I had just come back
from an inspiring walk in the woods and were lying on the bed
having some sweet pillow talk. Those are the moments I cher-
ish. Just the two of us—no agenda—reconnecting after a busy
week and unconcerned about the world outside our cocoon.

And then it happened. I would say it caught me off guard,
but that would be an understatement. There is no on guard for
what happened next. Men have feared it for centuries. It is the

inquiry that caused the term "blank stare" to be uttered for the first time. The question for which there is no plausible answer.

Einstein couldn't solve it... cavemen thought it was smarter to go fight a tiger... Freud withered under its weight... Gandhi stopped eating ... Custer left the house and headed to Little Big Horn ... Van Gogh hacked off an ear.

Berneice wasn't even looking at me when she asked the question. We were both lying on our backs, looking up at the ceiling, and then she dropped it on me like a hydrogen bomb: "Which one of my friends do you find sexy?"

Many things happen in the moments that follow—all critical. You immediately realize that honesty is the worst option, yet your answer must contain enough truth to be credible. Only three seconds have passed, but it seems like a month.

You quickly run through the checklist of bad options, your thought process interrupted by the faces of her friends passing through your brain like water through a spaghetti strainer.

Do I actually spit out a name? What are the consequences of more than one name? Is she thinking close friends or just acquaintances? Is there any chance she would believe "None of them"? What name could I say that would be someone we won't see for a long time? Can I convincingly fake a seizure? How will I decorate my new apartment?

There are many good reasons why men have feared the question for ages. You understand whatever name you utter will make seeing that woman again with your wife present completely awkward. You'll try some polite conversation, but no matter what you say your wife will be thinking, "So, he finds her sexy."

Too much time is passing with my silence. I need to say something to buy more time. So I try the old reverse-question-stall-for-time pivot and ask, "Which one of MY friends do YOU find sexy?" As I suspected, it failed.

She knows my silence means there are indeed some of her friends I find sexy. Names are racing through my head like a dinghy trying to find a safe harbor. Saying none of them is not plausible, so which name will cause her the least grief?

Now the passing moments are getting uncomfortable. I'm starting to feel like a mouse in an owl cage. It's only been twenty seconds, but I've developed hives. She's waiting for an answer; time is not my friend.

Suddenly I realize I may be able to buffer my answer with a disclaimer: finding an unacceptable flaw in the person whose name I utter. "Well, Penelope (no way I'm putting a real name in this column) is kind of sexy, but I could never be with a woman who saves her toenail clippings." My male brain is thinking, with that disclaimer I avoid the clumsy confrontation when we see Penelope.

Somehow in a moment of clarity I remember Rule 127 in the *How to Be a Man* handbook: *If your wife ever asks you which one of her friends you find sexy, try and say something enlightened about all women.*

I mumble, "Well, in their own way, they're all sexy." Berneice looks over at me like I've got cauliflower growing out of my forehead. She didn't need to say a word. I sheepishly looked away and played my last card. "I'll go fix dinner."

HOT PRETZEL

A few years ago I injured my back, and it resulted in some nerve damage. My enlightened neurologist recommended hot yoga to help stimulate regeneration and increase flexibility. It's funny, because during our time together, I genuinely thought my doctor liked me.

It was disturbing to open my eyes only to see a big, sweaty foot right in front of my face. It took a moment for me to realize it was mine.

I've started taking yoga. Not just any yoga, but *hot yoga*. It's where they turn up the heat and the humidity enough to cook shrimp. You start sweating when you walk through the door, so not only does yoga posing make you a pinch of salt away from being a pretzel, now you're a beer.

People who take hot yoga swear by it. They'll tell you that you'll be more flexible than you've ever been. If you try and tell them that you already think you're pretty flexible, they'll have none of it. On the flexibility of yoga issue they are completely inflexible.

I went in with an open mind and really tight pants. Initially, I was concerned I would look like an idiot. I didn't know the poses, and I was significantly older than the other folks who looked much better than me in really tight pants.

The instructor told me I only needed to "find my own shape." (Octagonal came to mind.) She said I didn't need to know all the traditional yoga poses. Figuring them out would come in time, so for now all I needed to do was get close and try not to fall over.

If you want to get a feel for all the possible yoga poses, throw yourself down a flight of stairs. By the time you hit bottom, you probably will have experienced twelve of them.

For the uninitiated here are a few of my favorites.

The Twisted Sage: You sit on the floor with one knee bent and pull your bent leg behind you. Then you twist your head as far as you can in the other direction so that you're looking over your opposite shoulder. Imagine Linda Blair without the soup. If your job requires you to face north and look south at the same time, then the Sage is your pose.

The Eagle: This one has you standing up straight on one leg. Your other leg wraps around your standing leg with your foot locking to the back of your calf. Meanwhile your arms are locked in front of you like two snakes intertwined. You're coiled up so tight there's a fifty-fifty chance they'll have to unwind you with a spatula. If any part of you comes loose, you could break a window. People trying to get out of this pose is the third-leading cause of death in America. There's cancer, heart disease, and people trying to get out of the Eagle pose.

The Standing Bow: Yeah, you guessed it. Stand on one leg and pull the other leg straight up, holding your ankle with one hand while your other arm points straight out. You're supposed to look just like a bow and arrow. I haven't gotten all the way to bow and arrow. My body settled more into slingshot. (Try and get that image out of your head.)

The Cat: This one is actually my favorite, mostly because I can do it. Down on all fours with your head up and back arched. It's a breathing pose, and unless you are right behind someone doing the Downward Dog (look it up for visual reference), it's a great way to loosen up.

Despite leaving class looking like I spent a week working in a prison laundry, I really am more flexible. I've gotten over not being able to pose like the other yogites in the class. When I see my classmates, I utter a confident "Namaste" instead of "Howdy." But mostly I've embraced a place where I can experience flop sweat, fall flat on my face, and have both be a sign that I'm making progress. That hasn't happened since I left public office.

MY PATIENT TEACHER

This Father's Day column made me realize how far our words can reach. It was passed along to folks all over the world. I heard from people who experienced loss as far away as China, New Zealand, and Russia. It helped me understand that grief is shared. While it seems profoundly lonely, it's really understood far beyond our hearts.

I've been thinking about taking the clothes out of my son's dresser. It's been three years since he passed away, and the folks who know something about these things tell me it would be the healthy thing to do. I'm not quite ready—still trying to process him being gone.

Seeing your child's headstone is about as real as it gets. While fathers who have lost children are members of the worst club ever, we manage to keep moving forward and along the way learn more about life and love than we ever imagined possible. Most of all, we've discovered that holes in the heart are the hardest holes to fill.

Our stories are different: a stunningly tragic auto accident . . . aspirating while sleeping . . . a deadly bout of pneumonia. We learned it doesn't matter if we see it coming or if it happens in an instant—the reality is the same. I was blessed to be holding my son in my arms when he left us. Others weren't so lucky. One dad was in Europe and was called by family friends. Police told another. And in those dreaded moments, they both immediately turned to nurture their other children. In the midst of their grief, they were fathers first. Through the haze of loss is the crystal-clear reality that mothers, brothers, and sisters all suffered the same loss.

It's like trying to wrap your arms around the ocean—it's just too big to comprehend, so you just give in to the waves and try not to go under.

I'd like to tell you about my son Zachary. He was an old soul. Cerebral palsy twisted his body but not his spirit.

He needed wheels to get around and a tube to eat (although, against doctor's orders, I would feed him sweet potato pie because he loved it). He didn't say words, but he spoke. He communicated perfectly—just differently.

He was wise beyond his years and knew how to smile through his challenges.

Zach was abled, not disabled. In fact, he may have been the most abled kid I've ever known. I've never understood labeling as "disabled" people who each day overcome challenges we can't even fathom. Hopefully, one day that bulb will go on over society's head.

Zach did his part to help enlighten. In 1985, he was one of five abled students to force the school board to allow mainstreaming in every school. Now kids with wheelchairs sit next to kids in regular chairs, helping to break down the social barriers that separated them.

We treated Zach no differently from our other sons. We always believed not treating him special was the best gift we could give him. It was our normal.

When he was young, I would dream about what he might have been like if he could walk and talk like other kids, and in time I realized how incredibly selfish that was. Zach was who he was, and like every other kid, he deserved to be loved in the package he came in. I never knew a walking, talking Zachary and in time grew to understand how unimportant those attributes were.

The only Zachary I knew was the one right in front of me, and in our eyes he was perfect. His brothers loved him, and he loved his brothers. It was our special brand of normal.

Zach was a patient teacher. If you were open to how he taught, there was much to learn. I remember a walk where I stopped to talk to a neighbor. I thought I had locked Zach's wheelchair, but in a flash he was rolling down a steep sidewalk slope, and I was in pursuit. I remember so clearly his arms waving, and I could hear him laughing. He was loving the ride—the bumps, the speed, and the wind. The fact that he was heading for a mailbox was of no concern. Life lesson: enjoy the journey, and don't worry about the destination. He would give you one of those gems every day—you just had to be willing to receive it.

Every midnight, I would go into his bedroom for one final check and to say goodnight. Those were our best times. I would whisper in his ear that I was going to shake him, and he would start to smile. A few shakes, and he would laugh. If you want to guarantee sweet dreams, make laughing with your son the last thing you do before you go to bed.

I can't even count the endless hours we would sit on the couch holding hands and watching Cubs games and bad westerns. He had the sweetest, softest hands.

Every day I see the worn-out spot on our leather couch where he rested his head.

I suppose this would be the point in this column where I would tell you to go hug your kids and tell them how much you love them because you never know. But that's not what Zach taught us. Just being normal was the lesson.

Take one more walk together . . . go throw the football one more time . . . sit on the porch and help them solve one more dating crisis. All the fathers I talked to miss their boys more than they can stand, but none of them regrets their time together. Just be normal.

Today I'm going to be thinking about a couple of other fathers whom I admire, and I know they'll have the same lump in their throat as I will. You can make yourself crazy wanting just a few more minutes with someone you've lost. Just one more slice of sweet potato pie, just one more inning of a Cubs game while holding a sweet hand. I know one day I'll take Zach's clothes out of his dresser. I'm just not going to do it today. I'm pretty sure Zach would be okay with that, and he would tell me not to worry about the mailbox, just enjoy the wind.

HEARING AIDS

Hearing aids are a big part of our family lore. My brother Greg; his wife, Sharon; and their son, Cameron, all sell them. My dad was in the business as well. So we don't take hearing aids lightly. Because he's in the business, my brother always gets the latest and coolest hearing aid. It's hard to use the word cool when describing a hearing aid, but if you're in the business it fits. The latest newfangled model inspired this column.

I was standing in the kitchen when, for no apparent reason, Berneice asked me to please poke a carp with ham. I calmly looked at her and said, "Honey we don't have a carp or a ham, and why on earth would I poke it if we did?" Berneice looked at me with that special look I've come to appreciate and began slowly mouthing the words with increased volume, "Please open the jar of jam."

My brother Greg is a hearing-aid distributer for a big chunk of North Florida. He has for years encouraged me to have my hearing checked. My answer is usually, "What?"

He's told me about cool new hearing aids that you can't even see. It's not so much about vanity for me. I've accepted with aging that things sometimes fall off, so I'm good with subtraction. I'm just not sure I'm at the point where I need to start adding things. Perhaps one day I'll reconsider, but for now I don't feel like I need new hearing aids, even if they make a new fancy model.

My brother fitted my ninety-one-year-old father with a set that has all the bells and whistles, which apparently my dad can now hear. I thought it was a bit cruel. My dad is finally at the age where he has a medical excuse for not listening to my eighty-nine-year-old mother. It seemed grossly insensitive of my brother to fix that for Dad, but I guess it's an acceptable trade-off to be able to hear Cubs games with more clarity.

Dad's new hearing aids are directly synced up with his phone via Bluetooth, so when he answers his phone, they fire up and the entire call is in his ears. It's a pretty good plan right up until my mom answers Dad's phone. Mom occasionally forgets that only Dad can hear his calls. That's when the fun begins.

Mom: *Hello.*

Me: *Dad, Mom is answering your phone by mistake.*

Mom: *What? I can't hear you. Who is this?*

Me: *I'm sorry, Dad.*

Mom: *I'm very busy. Whoever this is, you need to speak up. HELLO! WHO IS THIS?*

I picture my dad with his hands on his ears thrashing from side to side like he's standing next to the speakers at a Kiss concert.

Me: *Dad, Mom forgot your hearing aids are tied into the phone. You have to go get your phone from her.*

Mom: *HELLO! HELLO!*

Me: *Seriously, Dad, the yelling is not going to stop until you track her down.*

I visualize my dad wandering through the house like Frankenstein's monster . . . stiff legged and stumbling over furniture . . . hands extended out . . . unable to form actual words because a 747 is landing in his head.

Mom: (trying to figure out if she hit the right button on the phone) *HOLD ON. LET ME LOOK AT THIS PHONE!*

I realize that telling my mom to stop yelling is futile because only my dad can hear me. So I use the time to try and help him find her.

Me: *Dad, she may be upstairs. But don't yell for her because she'll yell back. You just need to go upstairs and grab your phone.*

Mom: *Oh, for the love of God, these new phones aren't worth a crap.*

Me: *Hang in there, Dad. It's a small house.*

Mom: *WHOEVER THIS IS, YOU NEED TO CALL BACK!*

Me: *I love you, Dad. I'll call back later.*

Look, I know hanging up was an option, but when you write a humor column you just can't let these moments pass. Maybe one day I'll give in and get a fancy pair of hearing aids. People who have them say they're life changing. At least that's what I've heard.

BILLY LOPP'S BRILLIANT IDEA

When you write a column for a family newspaper, you find yourself tiptoeing up to a pretty clearly drawn line when it comes to family content. But life sometimes happens on the other side of that line. This column was one of those times. When our friends shared that they were considering a home equity loan to cover their skyrocketing water bill, it started a flood of memories for me.

My friends have a twelve-year-old son who hasn't wanted to take a bath since . . . well, ever. Now he takes four showers a day. His father understands it's the same thing I learned from having three boys: the kid found it.

Go ahead, look away. This is one of those hard-to-confront subjects. It shouldn't be, but it is. Look, I understand. It is what happens to boys. There is an early moment of discovery. Our two-year-old grandson had to wear his onesie backward because his parents couldn't get him to keep his hand out of his pants. For boys, their penis is a playground. It's the monkey bars with their own private monkey.

The truth is men are fixated. While we aspire to a higher calling when it comes to matters of the loins, we are still cats chasing a shiny object. Our days are often driven by the hope of something good happening down there. It's nothing we're proud of, but it's true.

I discovered masturbation at the age of twelve. A visionary thirteen-year-old kid named Billy Lopp sat me and six of my friends down and explained the miracle he had recently discovered. I've forgotten the names of thousands of people in my life, but I will never forget Billy Lopp.

I remember thanking Billy and running home that day in the fall of 1965. If there was a record for running two and a half blocks, then I broke it. I headed straight for my bedroom in a dizzying mix of curiosity and wonder. I followed Billy's directions to the letter. I didn't come out of my room until 1972.

I couldn't imagine anything more fun. I quickly became the Monet of masturbators. I had turned it into an art form. I had discovered a new sport, and I didn't need to leave my room to participate.

My concern was the one cautionary note from Billy. You can only do it two thousand times in your life. Seriously, when you hear that from the expert on these matters, you believe it. At twelve years old, that seemed like a fair and plausible number.

So I had to lay out a plan. I figured I would want two kids, so my real number was 1,998. I would have to learn to carefully manage this finite number. My grandfather was sixty, so I guessed that would be about my life span. I tried dividing sixty years with an equal number for each year. That plan failed quickly. So I decided to just try and keep count and worry about it later.

I hit one thousand in record time. I had jumped out of the masturbation plane like I was wearing a knapsack instead of a parachute. I lost track after that because the idea of having children in the future quickly fell to second place on the masturbatory priority chart. I can't remember the exact moment I realized that Billy was wrong about the two thousand limit, but I'm guessing it was somewhere near age twelve and a half.

In a way there is something beautiful about the simplicity of a boy's pleasure. To find so much joy in a five-minute shower is a gift. With the full recognition of my own experiences, I carefully considered how to deal with the issue when it came to our boys. Do you have a responsible conversation or just let nature take its course? I opted for the vague "It's okay, just keep it to yourself" plan. What's interesting is what seemed great to me as a kid seemed unthinkable when it came to our boys. Not knowing where or when was much easier than confrontation.

So now when our friend's kid announces he's taking his fourth shower of the day, our advice is simple: increase the sound on your TV, and try to smile when you get your water bill. Boys will be boys, especially when they meet their own Billy Lopp.

BUBBLE ART

While I love writing humor, I've found that some of my favorite columns are about our journey through life—the places we go, the people we meet, and how we manage to traverse the path we find. I think a lot about life things. I think it's important to take notice as they go whizzing by.

With the promise of wind in his hair, my friend Neil Rambana climbed into his newly restored 1970 Datsun Roadster and was off to meet the tree frog that would jump in his lap—and the telephone pole that would be the new home for his dream car.

Neil spent more than a year restoring his Datsun: piece by piece, bolt by bolt, all from the ground up. I need two friends to help me bake a quiche, so I marveled at the feat.

He would send updates along the way. A snapshot of the dash with an exposed web of wires, and weeks later an engine tucked in place. Sometimes it would be something small, like a wooden gearshift knob. Finally, after two years came a picture of Neil standing next to his silver and red-topped masterpiece. Neil was Sir Edmund Hillary on top of Everest. He had planted his man flag in his new front seat. I'm pretty sure his grand plan wasn't to wrap his hard work around a phone pole, but it gave Neil a chance to experience something special.

A few years earlier a DVD produced by the magician Criss Angel caught my eye at a store. The DVD would reveal Angel's secret to levitation. Really? Was I only $19.95 away from floating above mere mortals? The possibilities were staggering—disrupting meetings, visiting churches, and rising up during sermons . . . an endless idea stream of how to abuse a new gift.

Of course, I knew it was a trick. If he could really levitate, I'm pretty sure he would have made the evening news by now. But I'm the guy who orders a food dehydrator at 3:00 a.m., so whipping out my credit card for a mystical power that would alter the course of life as I know it seemed reasonable. So, $19.95 later I had the DVD in hand. I went home, closed my office door, glanced up at the ceiling to make sure my path was clear, and fired it up. It took about a minute before Angel acknowledged he didn't ACTUALLY leave the ground.

Duh!

But here's the thing. For just a split second when the DVD was loading, I thought, "What if I paid $19.95 for a split second of 'what if' and it was worth every penny?" I've forgotten a million other moments, but I remember that one.

Fan Yang is a bubble artist off Broadway—way off Broadway. He creates giant bubbles with people and other crazy things inside. And in an instant they're gone. All his hard work—thousands of practice bubbles—bursting in failure. All his years of perfecting his art, only to amaze you with something that's gone in the blink of an eye.

Fan Yang understands that a moment matters.

Life has taught me to see the moments—even if fleeting—and to appreciate anticipation as its own gift. Amazing things—sometimes occurring in a flash—are so easy to miss: the first smile from a grandchild, the last "I do" at your kid's wedding, or seeing a couple kissing inside a big bubble off Broadway. The moments can be wonderfully happy or stunningly sad, but they define the difference between a well-lived life on a roller coaster and the predictable monotony of a merry-go-round. I'll take the roller coaster all day long.

I've thought a great deal about this roller coaster versus merry-go-round idea. I believe most people, when asked, would quickly choose the roller coaster because it seems more interesting. Sadly, it seems most folks, despite their interest in experiencing the ups and downs, sink into the safety and monotony of everyday life. Reality will do that to you sometimes: the rhythm of life swallowing us in a daily pattern morphing the special moments into life noise. I'm not a psychologist, but I play one in my own head, so I try to embrace those up and down moments.

As Neil learned, sometimes the moment is when a tree frog decides to come along for the ride. Neil proved he could take a punch even if it was from a tiny green fist, but building his dream car was now a footnote on a phone pole—years to build, a moment to enjoy, and an instant to lose.

Undaunted, Neil is starting over and restoring a Rolls-Royce because that's what roller-coaster people do. I can't wait for the first pictures. I'm guessing he'll start sending them any moment.

MIDLIFE DIET

Berneice and I are foodies through and through. I wish I had appreciated food when I was young enough to eat anything. Like life itself, food grows on you. Literally.

It's the oldest story in the book. Man falls asleep on couch. Man wakes up groggy and must have a bite of something sweet. Man has a forkful of pecan pie. Man heads to bed. Man stubs toe on grandson's toy fire truck. Man is now awake and must have a huge slice of pecan pie with ice cream to distract himself from throbbing toe. Man gains a pound.

We have all been there.

A few years ago I had an issue with my back and had to take steroids. Anyone who's taken steroids will tell you they can cause serious weight gain. I packed on forty pounds. I've gotten rid of most of it, but the last ten pounds have been a grind.

I've decided metabolism is unjust. In my twenties I could wolf down half a carrot cake for breakfast, skip lunch, and lose two pounds. I could get a chicken-fat IV and not gain weight. We didn't even think about it. Hit a drive-thru and get the giant cow burger with extra mayo, a puck of cheese, and a bucket of fries. It really didn't matter what it was—pounds slipped off like we were made of Teflon.

Today if I drive by a Wendy's, I gain a pound. Yesterday I thought about cheesecake and had to loosen my belt. This whole metabolism thing seems grossly unfair. You carefully monitor your intake—doing your best to knock out dairy, sugar, fried foods, calories—and you consider eating kale chips.

Seriously, kale chips? Thank you, but I'll have a bag of wall-paper instead.

So you spend all week giving up everything you really enjoy, and you lose three ounces. Then on Saturday you're out with friends, and you eat a buttered dinner roll and gain three pounds. You may as well just tell the waiter to bring you the "Make My Butt Lumpy" appetizer and, for the main course, a bowl of "I'll Hate Myself in the Morning."

I've tried a bunch of different diets with varying results. Atkins, all protein, was interesting. After ten days of eating meat you start evolving as a predator. My night vision improved, and I started developing pads on my hands and feet. A friend suggested the Mecca of meat eating: Fogo de Chão, a Brazilian restaurant/flesh factory. It was like eating on the Serengeti: skewer after skewer of everything dead. You didn't talk to your waiter—you growled. I surmised that heart doctors must have owned the place. I lost a little weight with Atkins but gained thirty pounds of bad karma, so I moved on.

I considered some of the plans where you spend your month digging into a big box of prepared meals sent to your door by Chef FedEx. "Hey, honey, how about a packet of lasagna tonight with a side of corn-on-the-carton?!" I simply couldn't reduce the joy of cooking to peeling off cellophane and punching in three minutes on the microwave.

Dr. Michael Mosley's Fast Diet was interesting. Two days a week you eat six hundred calories, and the other five days you eat pretty much what you want. The diet had potential until you realized that six hundred calories was basically a plum, a chicken wing, and a whiff of your neighbor's grill. Being happy for five days and surly for two didn't work for me.

I've decided that the best plan is to reason with my fat and treat it like my uncle Larry. I'm going to tell my fat that it needs to find somewhere else to live, that it needs to pack up its extra baggage and sublet someone else's midsection. If that doesn't work, I can always drop a quick ten pounds by selling the cat.

MURDER OF CROWS (OR WHY GOD MADE WINDOWS)

This column is a good example of reality trumping imagination, because it actually happened. I have this innate sense that there are things I'm supposed to like because I'm a man, but I just didn't get the gene. I applaud those who can do outdoor, deep-woods, gun-toting guy things. I simply choose to applaud from my sofa.

When it comes to the great outdoors, I've decided that my only weakness is that I have no strengths. I don't function well in the wild. My idea of camping is being as far away from the house as my longest extension cord. I consider essential camping equipment to be a twenty-four-inch flat screen and a carafe.

I'm an urban guy. Give me a week at a brownstone in Manhattan, and I'm in heaven. Nothing relaxes me more than the sound of a distant siren in the night. I'd rather kill a bottle of Merlot than a deer. I think the smell of grass is highly over-rated; warm hazelnuts on a street corner, now that's worth a whiff. I like the feeling of concrete under my feet. I wore a life jacket at Disney's It's a Small World.

Look, I have good friends who hunt. They'll wake up at 4:00 a.m. to go sit in a tree for five hours and wait for Bambi to stroll by, and they'll love every minute of it. One friend just got a cool new bow with a scope. I guess that evens the playing field a bit more, but I'm pretty sure Robin Hood would scoff at the contraption. Give Robin a scope and the Sheriff of Nottingham is toast.

If you take the whole killing-an-unarmed-creature out of the equation, I get the allure. The thrill of the hunt, hunter bonding, and shooting a cool gun all seem kind of fun. Responsible hunters eat what they kill. I do admire that. As nonhunters we are confronted with our hypocrisy. We have no problem buying a nice rib eye from the meat counter—we just don't want to do the dirty work.

Correct. I admit it: guilty as charged. I don't feel the need to raise chickens to eat an omelet or, for that matter, to drill a hole in the yard to get gas. I'm a gatherer.

One of my best friends, John Citron, moved to Missouri to live on a farm in the country. He loves it. He has become an avid hunter of all things. He's thrilled to prepare an entire game dinner. Teriyaki-marinated loin of deer and pan-fried pheasant. It was wonderful, and nothing screams fresh like picking the buckshot out of your appetizer. But I'll admit I looked over my shoulder before I ate to make sure I still saw the cat.

Citron loves every moment of his outdoor life. He relaxes by sitting on his pontoon boat and skipping .22 rounds off the surface of his lake. Not long ago I called him on a Saturday morning. He was sitting on his porch having coffee and enjoying the solitude of the farm. All of a sudden he yelled, "HOLD

ON!" and I heard the phone drop. Then three shots rang out, followed by a stream of expletives, and then, "Your day is coming, you SOB."

My first thought was that the country air had finally gotten to him and he was holding off the feds, but it turns out it was another chapter in his ongoing battle with a snapping turtle living in his pond. John is a national expert in sports marketing, a former world-class hurdler, and a sought-after track coach, but at that moment all I heard was Jed Clampett.

I've had a few adventures as friends and family have taken me hunting. My brother-in-law John has tried for twenty-five years to convert me to an outdoorsman. He has a hundred-acre farm in east Tennessee. On one trip, he provided me with a shotgun. He might as well have handed me a loaf of pumpernickel for all the good it would do, but I gripped it like a man and gave him a confident nod.

My wife, Berneice, has three other brothers, and along with one other guy (who just came along to see the goober Berneice married), they all joined in to round out the hunting party.

John thought I might enjoy hunting crow. As a former elected official, I had certainly eaten enough of it, so the idea of killing a few was plausible. We loaded our guns and headed out for our guy-a-thon.

We fought our way through the brush filled with what John calls "You ain't goin' no damn place" vines. Past the vines, we marched up a steep ridge, and you could hear the crows off in the distance. It was pretty cool. Next we had to find the best spot to blend into the brush and trees near the top of the ridge. Like chess pieces, we all crouched into our strategic positions.

I was really going to do it: I was going to aim a gun at something with the intent of hitting it. It was an entirely unexpected titillation. The liberal me was wrestling with the prehistoric me, like two emotional rats in a wool sweater. But there was no backing down. I was packing heat (which by the way was a lot heavier than I thought it would be).

The guys were all in camouflage gear, I was in a navy-blue Kenneth Cole brushed-leather windbreaker, but I pretended to blend in. Berneice's brother Paul was in charge of the crow-caller thing. He would blow a perfect cadence, and the crows would respond in kind. With each call you could hear the crows getting closer.

This was it: I was a hunter. My heart was beating through my chest. I was finally going to be a man's man in front of the Cox boys. I was getting hand signals from John. I have no idea what they meant, but I nodded back in affirmation and gave a closed-fist double pump with a two-finger chaser. I think in hand language I had told him I'd wet myself.

I felt the cold steel of the trigger. I could see my breath in the December air. The crows were about to appear over the ridge. We were at the ready. I rested my cheek against the stock and peered into the blue sky, waiting for the murder of crows.

At about that moment, my cell phone rang. The sound of crows gave way to "The Way You Look Tonight" by Frank Sinatra. It was Berneice checking to see how the hunt was going. I would have needed a courtroom artist to capture the look on John's face. His head was cocked instead of his gun. Paul was still blue from blowing the crow-caller, and the guy who was just there to see goober fell over laughing. Brother Bill suggested that in the future a crow-call ringtone might be smarter. Ouch.

Mother Nature will just have to learn to tolerate my occasional visits. I'm a guy who prefers a skyline to a tree line, and I'm entirely comfortable having Ruth's Chris kill my steak. I think there's something inside all of us that yearns for the great outdoors. I'm pretty sure that's why God made windows.

PASSWORDS

I got a flood of e-mails after this one. It seems I'm not the only lost soul in the password jungle.

This column will now be password protected. Passwords should contain some combination of the following: between eight and fifty-three letters/numbers/symbols including one uppercase letter, one number, one symbol from the line of symbols above the numbers on your keyboard, a common forest shrub, the first ingredient from a traditional kosher recipe, and the proper name of a saltwater fish.

Butterbutt1954$&#Huckleberry1/4cupchicken-schmaltzBluespottedboxfish

Sorry, that password has already been taken.

It seems today we need passwords to recover our passwords, and every website we visit has different criteria. So having just one universal password won't fly. We are forced to try to remember multiple combinations of silliness. There are sites where you can store all your passwords, but they require a master password. And that's the tip of the security iceberg.

Next are the "challenge questions." What was the nickname you gave your first car? What city would you like to live in if you like quiche? On which side of your neck did you get your first hickey? It's too much to remember.

Recently my dad was sent to a rehab facility for a few weeks to recover from a medical issue. Dad is a newshound and a sports nut, so disconnect him from the Internet for a few days and he gets pretty stir-crazy. So we wanted to get him set up with his computer. We fired up his laptop, and up popped his password prompt. We entered his password—and it failed. Again and again, it failed.

I asked my dad if he was 100 percent sure we had the correct password. "Yes, I'm sure. It's the number of my favorite baseball player reversed." All of a sudden I was Robert Preston. "Well, ya got trouble, my friend, right here, I say. Trouble right here in River City."

After going through every player on his favorite team's roster and reversing their numbers, the only thing we had gotten into was more trouble.

The reluctant next step was calling the folks who made his computer for some tech help. After thirty-four layers of voice prompts, I found myself on the phone explaining our problem to a very nice woman eight thousand miles away with a very thick East Indian accent. Repeatedly she told me "hoshifate very fast." Over and over she and I worked to overcome our language barrier. I was banging my head on the keyboard like I was trying to tenderize meat. After thirty dysfunctional minutes, I finally got it: hold shift and hit the eight key very fast.

That's it? With all the technology on the planet, the trick to getting into this computer was to hold one key and hit another really fast? After convincing myself this wasn't some elaborate prank, I started doing it. It was a two-handed job, so I put my phone on speaker and started banging the 8 key until my hand started to cramp. I must have hit the key five hundred times. I could feel a blister forming on my fingertip. My brow was covered in sweat from my finger-tapping marathon.

All of a sudden, I was overcome by a warm glow. Something was happening on the screen. I hugged a nurse like I had just gotten my colonoscopy results. The little hourglass on the screen was flipping over. I looked up, anticipating the release of confetti.

Wait for it . . . here it comes. It was all going to be okay. And then four words appeared on the screen under a little empty box: Please Enter Your Password.

Shoot me, please.

Look, is there any chance we could all just agree to trust each other? It really would be much easier. Seriously, I'm willing to remove all password protection from my bank accounts if all of you double-pinky-promise not to take my money. Hey, I'm not alone in this. I just got an e-mail from a guy I've never met in Nigeria. He's willing to give me access to his account if I send him mine. That sounds like a good start.

PORK VINDALOO

The only area of my life where I consider myself truly coura-geous is eating. I pretty much will try anything, and I will do it with gusto. However, courage loses some luster when you're curled up and begging for forgiveness. Nobody really cared too much about my feelings after this one.

For reasons I can't explain, I had somehow developed a nar-row view of Indian food. I lumped it in the "It won't like you, so don't like it" category. When it comes to food, I'm up for almost anything, so my unintended boycott of Indian food was never really well thought out. My eating history is filled with culinary left turns.

On a trip to Spain, my "eat anything" partner, David, and I pledged to eat the most ridiculous thing we could find on every menu. It was actually pretty wonderful. Our wives were supportive nonparticipants. I've learned I actually prefer parts from the front end of an animal, but the back end has its own appeal. The bounty from the middle is usually the safest, but when you're on an adventure, it's usually the outer boundaries that are the most interesting.

Years ago, Tallahassee chef extraordinaire Lucy Ho cooked a twelve-course meal for me, with each course relating to a month in the Chinese calendar. It was at that dinner that I bit into my first eye of lamb. (Maybe it was a goat; it was hard to tell because there was no head attached.) The eye and I looked at each other, and I went for it.

Recently I was in Washington, DC, for a quick two-day trip. My friend Reggie tried to get me into what's generally regarded as the best Indian restaurant in the city, but with short notice we found ourselves at the next best thing: a new trending Indian place in Georgetown.

It took one bite for me to realize I'd been wrong. The food was amazing. It was a burst of cumin, yogurt, and cilantro. How did I miss out on this explosion of flavors for so many years? I tried to catch up in one night and left the place stuffed.

The next night I had an early flight, so I figured I'd stay close to the hotel. I happened to look out my window, and right across the street was the top-rated Indian restaurant we couldn't get into the night before. It was kismet, so I took a chance and scored a seat at the bar.

I told the waiter to just indulge himself and choose whatever he thought might be fun. He did, and each course was amazing. I had found Indian food, and I was in cumin heaven—right up until my 6:00 a.m. flight.

Here's a travel tip: if you're not used to Indian food, don't eat it two nights in a row and then fly early the next morning. It started quietly enough—a little stomach rumble, nothing serious. That lasted a few minutes, and then it hit.

It was clear that our flight was in trouble. Without the gory details, two flight attendants resigned, our flight was diverted to Knoxville, and seven passengers were offered free tickets to anywhere—for life. Children were crying. The guy next to me tried to open the window. I had a Jakarta traffic jam in my gut, and there was a cow in the middle of the intersection.

Many questions passed through my mind.

How could I have been this stupid? How could I have knowingly put lava in my gut? Why had a jackal crawled up inside me and died? Why was I Linda Blair? Is it possible to swallow hot coals? How has India survived this long as a country? Is it illegal to spit fire on an airplane? If I explode, will I still get my frequent flier miles? Was Gandhi truly contemplating, or was he just quietly passing gas?

I'm positive nobody wants to hear the end of this adventure. (Seriously, you don't.) So I'll leave you with an old Indian proverb: It is little use to dig a well after the house has caught fire.

I don't know which Indian said that, but I'm pretty sure he or she just had eaten pork vindaloo.

THE McTRUTH

I love to people watch. Despite all the whizz-bang electronic distractions in our world, there is nothing I find more interesting than folks just being folks. This encounter in America's heartland was a classic that I thought needed to be shared.

The fight to allow same-sex marriages was over long before it got to the Supreme Court.

America had already made its decision. All the Supreme Court did was put a stamp on it.

There's a McDonald's right off Highway 60 in Mountain Grove, Missouri, smack-dab in the middle of America. If you spend any time in that part of our country, you know the main crop is brutal truth. They don't mix words, and there's no space between their hearts and their lips. If they think it, they say it.

Last Sunday morning over coffee and McMuffins, four guys with blue jeans, boots, and "CAT" hats held court. Allan Wiese was the leader, but he'd tell you he's nobody special. Every Sunday morning, he and his friends—Duane, Herschel, and Ben—get together to talk politics. The same seats, the same coffee, every Sunday.

Until I showed up, the only audience beyond their table was the pimple-faced kid behind the register. If you want the unvarnished truth, you only need to go as far as Allan Wiese's table. It was perfect heartland theater with a side of hash browns.

With a deliberate cadence and a handful of newspaper, Wiese began reading the Supreme Court decision on same-sex marriage, giving meaning to every word. He ran into a word that was unfamiliar, stared for a moment, and in the most unaffected way said to his guys, "That's a word I don't know, but it looks like it could be important," then he moved on. The honesty was refreshing. When he finished the read, it was time for the verdict.

His first comment—"Hillary and her friends will be thrilled"—had me waiting for the other shoe to drop. And then he surprised me. Even though "Hillary and her friends" weren't his cup of McCoffee, he was 100 percent supportive of what the court had ruled. He could care less about same-sex marriage, and that's the point. What he cared about was personal freedom.

There are folks who will go to their graves never understanding how the court could make this ruling, and there are those who will never understand why it took so long. But like every campaign in American history, winning isn't about the two sides that have already made up their minds—it's about the people sitting on the fence. That's the way it's always been.

Same-sex marriage became a legal reality not simply because it was just. It became law because the people who don't care about same-sex marriage finally spoke up. People like Allan Wiese have more important things to worry about than trying to convince folks that the bedroom is the only room in a home.

Allan Wiese was all in on what the Supremes did because he figures if government can tell other folks how they can live their lives, then it's just a slippery slope to his front door and those matters that are important to him. He found his own path to justice, and it had nothing to do with two guys sharing a wedding cake.

The Supreme Court ruling wasn't about sexual preference—it was about personal freedom. The only mystery is why it took so long to bring equity to the lives of good people whose only request was fairness. America got there a long time ago. It just took a while for it to make its way up to the ivory tower.

MY SECRET SHAME

This column was very cathartic. I needed to share this . . . to purge my soul . . . to admit my unholy dependency.

I have a secret shame. There, I admit it. I think we all do. That one thing we do we're not proud to share, but we just can't help ourselves. That one bad habit, the sinful indulgence. The one thing we don't want anyone else to know about.

It's usually not a bad thing, probably just something you're not thrilled for others to know. Maybe it's opening the refrigerator at 2:00 a.m. and eating leftovers like a mountain lion. I've got a friend who occasionally pees off his back porch. He says it makes him feel free. I'm here to share, not judge. Although it has caused me to rethink the amount of time I spend on his porch.

I asked around my office if folks would be willing to share their secret shame. I wish I hadn't. We have a private Pringles stasher and another who cleans her ears with a bobby pin. Another can only go to the bathroom with his shirt off. It's my fault for asking, and I quickly realized we really don't need to know each other that well.

So here is mine: Steven Seagal movies. I realize there are few things less redeeming than ninety minutes of Seagal, but I can't help it. His movies are like driving by a traffic accident: they're horrible, but you have to look.

Berneice won't go there. Not even a little. It's not like I meant to live in the Seagal closet, but if I suggested to Berneice that we should watch one of his films, I would be politely dismissed as she responds by extending the word *really* to eleven seconds. She would rather check the neighbor's dog for fleas than lower her standards to the depths of Seagalism.

Seagal movies are so bad that they're good. Tough guys in the movies are supposed to know how to hold a gun. Not Seagal. When he holds one, he looks like he's carrying a dirty diaper to a pail.

He does have a unique skill set. Not many guys know how to self-acupuncture while disarming a nuclear weapon. In Seagal movies, there is never a bank robber. A foil that mundane would never get his attention. The bad guy needs to be blowing up the planet or at least Cleveland. The president has to be held hostage in a submarine, or a train full of nuns must have dynamite strapped to their habits. It has to be so cataclysmic that failure dooms us all.

At some point in his movies, the secretary of defense—surrounded by our finest military minds—realizes he can't handle the task and discovers Seagal is already on site posing as a pastry chef. They either have to pay the bad guy ten gazillion dollars or hand over the fate of the world to Seagal.

Inevitably, Seagal will be in the middle of a bad-guy circle. Ten guys with pitchforks and axes. He's armed with a credit card. Within seconds he will have swiped them all into submission. Why they all go after him one guy at a time is beyond me, but I'm guessing they don't have a bad-guy circle meeting before they attack.

After he gets through the army of bad guys, he ends up face-to-face with the head bad guy, some actor slightly below him on the "I'll do anything" movie circuit, like Kris Kristofferson. Despite the head bad guy having a shotgun, Seagal manages to finish him off with a salad fork (I'm pretty sure he has a concealed utensil permit).

Finally, we see the female lead, usually a 1970s version of Kelly Le Brock. Despite having been tied to a chair for a week, she stands perfectly coiffed and stumbles over bodies to fall into his arms.

And . . . scene.

I've tried to examine what it is that draws me to this dribble. I'm a smart guy. Why am I so willing to waste ninety good minutes of my life? I know I'm not proud of it because I won't admit it to Berneice. If she calls from out of town and asks what's up, I tell her I'm watching CSPAN. I don't want her to think less of me.

Maybe we just need the occasional mindless indulgence to flush out the hair in our brain drain. Or perhaps we need to see what's really bad to get a perspective on what's really good. I don't know.

What I do know is this: five hours after Berneice leaves town, I turn into a caveman. I pick up food in a Styrofoam container and, with knuckles dragging on the ground, I make my way to the television and search for Seagal. I'm not proud of it, but at least I take comfort in the knowledge that somewhere there's a group of nuns who are safe tonight.

NO JOKE

This is one of my favorite columns. I think that's because I can actually picture Sonny Glass. Sitting with him is a rich ethnic smorgasbord of joy.

A new convict is sitting in the prison lunchroom with an old convict. From across the room, someone yells, "Forty-six," and everyone starts laughing. A few minutes later someone yells, "Thirty-nine," and again the whole room cracks up. The new convict asks what's so funny, and the old convict explains that they've all been there so long everybody knows the jokes, so they gave them numbers just to save time. A few minutes later someone yells, "Fifty-six," and nobody laughs. The new convict asks why not, and the old convict says, "Some guys just don't know how to tell a joke."

I've never been any good at telling jokes. If it's a good one, I can't get through it without laughing because I know the punch line. More often, it's my inability to get it right. "Two nuns and a plumber were walking down the street. No, wait, it was one nun and two insurance salesmen. No, no they weren't walking, they were in a cab . . ." You've pretty much lost your audience by then.

My friend Sonny Glass, a former stand-up comedian turned stand-in rabbi, told me the prison joke. His delivery was flawless, his timing impeccable. His cadence rising and falling, his exuberant hands and shoulder shrugs were perfectly in rhythm with the story. What took me a few sentences to write took Sonny five minutes of character development, which was as funny as the punch line.

I'm okay hearing a good joke, although when the telling begins I feel a twinge of social pressure to laugh at the punch line even if it's not funny. I admit the extent of my laughter is directly proportionate to the warmth I feel for the joke teller. Good joke tellers are telling the joke because they think it's funny and they want to share. When a joke is used to just cover an otherwise awkward moment, it's not so funny.

I've always found real life provides the best material. My parents are hysterical, and they never tell a joke. Mom's eighty-eight years old, and Dad is ninety. Their everyday life provides more than enough humor. Last week I had tears in my eyes from hearing them share their common complaint about the toilets at my brother's house being too short. Gravity took care of them sitting down; getting up was an entirely different story. Hearing Mom explain how she had to try and stand up from such an awkward position was priceless.

Mom: (in her best Jewish Mother delivery) *Who does that? Who makes a toilet that short without a bar to grab on to? A handle, a hook, an ejector seat—anything to get me off this thing. Everybody else's toilet seats are normal size, but no, not your brother's. It's like I was superglued to the seat. All I could do was scream for your father and pray he had his hearing aids turned on. Otherwise they'll have to pry me off this seat with a spatula.*

The best part is hearing Dad laugh while hearing Mom tell me the story. They crack each other up. On debating whether to drive or fly to a recent wedding:

Dad: *I can't fly with her anymore. She can't get from one plane to the other. It's like the guy whose friend had a heart attack and died on the second hole of their golf game—hit the ball and drag Larry, hit the ball and drag Larry. That's what it's like at the airport.*

Mom: *He wants to put me on a meat hook like a butcher uses for a cow. Just hoist me up and slide me from terminal C to terminal B.*

Priceless.

I know I'm not revealing some secret clinical theory when I share the old adage "Laughter is the best medicine." I have forgotten a thousand times when I was upset about something, but I have a tangible memory of the times we've laughed so hard we couldn't breathe. I love those contagious moments when you're laughing as you share something and the person you're telling it to starts laughing as hard as you before they even know what you're laughing about. It seems laughing is funny all by itself.

I recall years ago waking up from a dream where I hit my mother in the head with a golf ball. (This would not be a good time to examine the dream—let's just go with it.) In my dream, Mom was a couple of hundred yards ahead of me in a golf cart. I hit my drive, and in slow motion I could see the ball and Mom on a collision course. When the ball hit her, it made that "cluck" sound you hear when you pop your tongue from the roof of your mouth. (Go ahead and try it—it makes the story better.)

I woke up laughing hysterically, which in turn woke Berneice up. I remember so clearly how hard she was laughing without a clue as to why. The fact that I couldn't catch my breath enough to share the ridiculous dream wasn't important—my laughter caused her laughter. When Berneice laughs uncontrollably, it's a beautiful thing. I'm pretty sure that if I woke her up and tried to tell her a joke, this story wouldn't have been worth sharing.

I'm not anti-joke, I'm pro-funny—so if a joke gets you there, that's great. I'm just more of a real-life guy. I've been sharing newspaper space with readers for almost three years, and during that time many have shared with me the things that make them laugh—their stories, their spontaneous adventures, life material. Keep on sharing.

I'm going to try and laugh even more in the upcoming year. It's a much more achievable resolution than going to the gym five days a week, and I don't have to look at the stocky dude in the one-size-too-small bike shorts to achieve my goal.

A guy hears a knock on his door. When he opens it, there's no one there. He looks down and sees a snail, picks it up, and throws it across the street into the neighbors' yard. Two years later, there's a knock on his door. He opens the door, and the snail looks up and yells, "What the hell!"

I'll be here all week, folks. And don't forget to order the veal.

PILLOW SPEAKERS

This is one of those little adventures that remind me how much I love Berneice. Despite the absurdity of my idea, she dove right in. I asked for pillow speakers for Christmas so I could try this plan. Even though she never thought for a moment it might work, she stuffed my stocking with everything I needed and walked away. I suppose when you've heard enough of my goofy ideas, you develop a rhythm about how to respond.

The funniest thing about this column is that folks shared with me that they enjoyed having to look up the French translations. It was a kind of delayed gratification.

I was sitting outside a small café in Paris, having a friendly chat with a couple I had just met. I recall it being a crisp, sunny afternoon as I sipped my espresso. Without warning, a guy I had never met came up behind me and started smacking me around with a day-old baguette. I woke up.

I'm in the midst of a grand experiment. I'm trying to learn French while I sleep. Seriously, I am. I've actually thought about doing this for some time, but when I recently saw a video on YouTube titled "Learn French While You Sleep," it seemed like it matched up pretty well with my idea.

So I began doing the type of analytical scientific research you should do before introducing a potentially dynamic influence to your brain: I Googled it. I learned that in a study by the Weizmann Institute of Science in Israel, scientists were able to condition subjects to associate smells with certain sounds even while they were asleep.

The researchers concluded, "This acquired behavior persisted throughout the night and into ensuing wake, without later awareness of the learning process. Thus, humans learned new information during sleep."

Hey, then why not French?

So I bought myself a set of pillow speakers—yes, they make them, little speakers that plug into your tape recorder and broadcast only to you through your *oreiller*. (Sorry, these French words pop into my head without warning.)

Next I set out to find the best French tutorial on tape. I found one with just the words directly translated. The guy on the tape says the English word, then follows with the same word in French. Nothing else, just straight word to word. After a few nights, my concern began to grow that my brain might not get the sequence. The guy on the tape says "angel," then "*l'ange*." The next word is "aardvark." Since I'm sleeping, I don't know when my brain kicks in. What if my brain is hearing the French word first? Now I'm in France telling some guy his wife looks like an aardvark.

So I started looking for a tape that was more conversational, something that had a bit more relevance, like if I needed *la toilette*. (Sorry, can't help it.)

I found a book on tape with a couple who simply chat with each other, first in English and then the same conversation in French. The lessons are designed to give the listener a more rhythmic approach to grasping a new language. So a couple of weeks ago I shifted to this approach.

The problem is I've started dreaming about this couple. I'm pretty sure some French words are getting through, but I find myself deeply invested in these two. I was in a meeting yesterday and found myself wondering what they were up to today. Good Lord, my awake brain has me eavesdropping on two people who don't even exist because my sleeping brain is an *imaginaire harceleur*!

I'm not giving up. This brain intrusion isn't leading me to turn French, although when the dream attacker came at me with the baguette, I did immediately surrender. I'm going to find a tutorial somewhere between the minimalist approach of simple one-word repetition and moving in with Marie and Claude Bonaparte. I'm still convinced there is some merit to this approach. Either way it seems harmless. It's not like I'm trying to learn how to install a gas oven while I'm sleeping.

So if you run into me and I drop a little *fumier de cheval* on you, you'll know I found it in my sleep.

ROAD TRIP

Traveling always has its own set of baggage. We love getting wherever it is we are going, but the allure of the trip has gotten less interesting over the years. I have a feeling there is a cross-country adventure in our future—just not quite yet.

I'm considering all the cool stops we could plan into a cross-country road trip: seeing the four-legged lady, the man with the lion's face, and the world's biggest bag of hair. And that's just our family—imagine what else is out there!

I define a real road trip as at least five states. We can't remember the last time we took a real road trip—just the two of us in a car full of music, not knowing what's around the bend but excited to find out. The romance of a road trip is enough to cloud the reality.

It's easy to forget the boys in the backseat drawing the uncrossable imaginary line marking their territory, and the inevitable battle when one would cross into the demilitarized zone. The I-have-to-pee-but-we-just-stopped-five-minutes-ago moments. The Dad-I-think-the-pecan-log-made-me-sick stops. One trip got so bad I stopped the car, got out, and started walking to Tallahassee. We were in Tennessee.

We tend to remember the laughs, the bonding, and all the vistas along the way. So now, twenty years later with the kids long gone, Berneice and I are considering packing up the car and driving each other crazy.

So here's the trip. Our friends John and Liz are gaining a son-in-law in their hometown of Mountain Grove, Missouri. We helped raise their daughter Riley, and there's no way we're missing this wedding.

Mountain Grove is a perfectly quaint little town of 4,623 in the Show-Me State. Dr. Todd's Dental Office (that's not a description, it's the actual name), Bushwackers Hair Salon, I Do Interior Painting (again, that's the name), and Soggy Bottom Plumbing are all part of the thriving business sector. But after searching the local motel selection, I found myself Googling "Bates" to see if there was one nearby as an alternative.

We finally decided the better bet was to see what was available in the thriving metropolis of Cabool, just nine miles up the road. After all, Cabool has a winery, so they must have a couple of interesting places to stay. Cabool, Missouri, strikes me as an odd place for a winery, but nothing says flamboyant like a good midwestern wine (a buttery-smooth marriage of wild berries and oak with just a hint of badger).

After sifting through the two lodging options in Cabool, we chose the America's Best Motel. (I mean if it's America's best, it must be pretty good.) They had two nonsmoking rooms, one with a king-size bed and the other with two doubles. We asked for the king, but it was taken. Really?

We took the doubles, and I asked if they could e-mail me the confirmation. The "I think we can" response led me to ask for the confirmation number while on the phone. "Sure, not a problem. It's sixty-eight."

When your confirmation number is sixty-eight, it starts you thinking. It can't possibly be the number of rooms they've rented. Did they reach one thousand and decide to start over? Are they just picking random numbers like a bingo barker? If we make it out of Cabool, I'll let you know.

So here we are confronted with the road-trip dilemma. Do we embrace the four-day adventure?

Are America's roads still innocent with roadside eclectic markets selling Jimmy Carter peanut mugs, or will this be a seventyish-miles-per-hour interstate trudge across half the country, stopping only for road construction traffic jams? Maybe we should just hop on a plane and spend the extra time sipping fine wine at the Cabool Country Club and getting a bouffant at Bushwackers? It's a close call.

If you see us at Gate 3B, stop and say howdy. We'll let you know what we decided.

THE GOOGLE

My mother is a treasure trove of columns. My greatest challenge is resisting the temptation to write about her every week. Mom is a living, breathing Neil Simon play.

My eighty-nine-year-old mother could hardly contain herself when she called to tell me she had found a place where she could get all kinds of senior discounts. When I asked where, she said, "The Google," as if it were a storefront located between Macy's and Publix.

Time to settle into the recliner because I know I'm not getting off this call anytime soon.

My mom is a fierce shopper. Put a parachute on sale, and Mom's all over it because it's not about need, it's about price. She'd buy a show pony to get a free harness. I've come to believe it's a recessive gene, and I may have gotten it.

If I hear the phrase "as seen on TV," I know I'm in trouble. I don't need the Pocket Garden Hose that shrinks into a fanny pack, but I really want one. Who wouldn't want the Bacon Bowl—wolf down some mac and cheese and clog an artery all in the same meal.

The Olde Brooklyn Lantern (which gave off as much light as bright teeth) and the Chillow (guaranteed to put you to sleep by freezing your head) were just two of my really smart purchases. But I'm drawn to these things like a moth to the Big Blue Bug Zapper (which by the way is buy one, get one free, in case you want to hear the sizzle in full stereo).

How can a person even get through a day without the Ankle Genie, the Head Wedgie, or the Long Reach Comfort Wipe (oh yeah, it exists)? Do you really want to head into the world today without having used your Wax Vac? That's right, you stick this vacuum in your ear (seems safe to me).

Now back to the Google. Dad is in the background using his electric razor. I know that because I'm on a speakerphone and it sounds like a B-52 is landing in their bedroom. With my buzzing father as the background music, the call went something like this:

Mom: *I found this place on the Google.*

Me: *What place?*

Mom: *A place where I can find senior discounts on every-thing like Kohl's and even Wendy's!*

Dad: (yelling from the background) *Like Kohl's.*

Mom: *I said that, Lenny.*

Me: *That's great, Mom.*

Mom: *Oh yeah, Belk* (where she's purchased every Christmas present since 1983), *the bagel place, and everywhere.*

Dad: *AND Kohl's!*

Mom: *He can't hear with that razor buzzing* (neither can the neighbors).

Me: (sensing this is about to take a turn for the worse) *What else, Mom?*

Mom: *Anything you can think of . . . food, places we eat* (apparently different than food), *and everywhere.*

Dad: *Even Wendy's!*

Mom: *I said Wendy's!*

Dad: (Wait for it . . . here it comes) *And Kohl's!*

Me: (with tears rolling down my cheeks) *What do you have to do to get the discounts?*

Mom: *You just have to be able to prove you're a senior* (as if pulling up to the counter on a scooter wasn't proof enough).

Dad: *You can get a discount on a bagel!*

Mom: *Delicious bagels and other food . . . I mean we are saving a fortune* (that's a lot of bagels).

Me: *Well, that's great, Mom. What's the name of the site?*

Mom: *Jim Hene . . . Hami . . . something like that.*

Me: *Did you bookmark the site so you can find it again?*

What follows is about ten seconds of silence. I hear the razor shut off, and I can just imagine the two of them looking at each other like two squirrels who just dropped a nut, visually confronting the harsh reality that they may not be able to find the site again.

When I was a kid, my brother fell out of the car going about one mile per hour in a parking lot. I calmly told my parents that Greg had fallen out of the car. It didn't register for a moment, but when it did I will never forget the look on their faces. That was the look I was imagining they were having as they pondered losing something slightly more important than Greg.

This just got real. After all, they had led full lives. If you can't get a discount bagel, is there really a reason to go on?

Not to worry, this is just the kind of challenge my parents live for. "Get the keys to the car, Lenny. We're going back to the Google!"

ACKNOWLEDGMENTS

Thanks to Bob Gabordi, executive editor of the *Tallahassee Democrat*, for reading my first column and asking if I could write another one. To my writing coaches and patient teachers Mary Ann Lindley, Julie Strauss Bettinger, and Randi Atwood. To my mother and father for their lives well lived and the endless stream of material they've provided. To Dustin and Jackson for keeping me grounded. To all my dear friends who have allowed me to show them the underside of a bus. To Kris, David, and Chuck for being my "Cleveland" friends.

To Zachary for showing me how to live my life with perspective.